More Praise for
Elvis: Precious Memories

"The real story about Elvis' life and death we have all been waiting for is here. After almost 20 years, we really get the inside story as told by two strong women that Elvis loved and respected. This book is the positive yet honest portrait of Elvis that fans all over the world have longed for. Now Elvis' memory will receive the dignity and understanding it deserves."

> —Priscilla Parker
> "We Remember Elvis"
> Fan Club President
> Pittsburgh, Pennsylvania

"In *Elvis: Precious Memories*, we meet Elvis the man. Through firsthand stories, we come to know the person behind the persona of the King of Rock 'n Roll...a kind man of extraordinary talent and uncommon generosity, rooted in deep family bonds.
"The authors have indeed shared a precious treasure...truly a gift for those of us intrigued by the Elvis mystique."

> —Donna C. Roberts
> TV Producer/President, NewVue Films
> Montreal, Canada

"Finally, Elvis' family breaks their silence and we are all blessed for their sharing with spellbinding and rare insights into what really went on behind the gates of Graceland and in the heart of the man behind its legend."

> —Dr. Judy Kuriansky
> Clinical Psychologist, Radio Talk Show
> Host, Author, Lecturer

"We at TCM for Elvis endorse the book *Elvis: Precious Memories* by the ones who loved and knew him best, his family...A book so long overdue, but never too late to show the real man behind the image."

> —Michelle Elaine, President
> TCM for Elvis*

*TCM (Taking Care of Memories) for Elvis is an international organization to uphold the name of Elvis Presley with integrity and respect.

Elvis: Precious Memories

ELVIS
Precious Memories

By Donna Presley Early and Edie Hand

with Lynn Edge

The Best of Times, Inc.
Birmingham, Alabama

Published by
THE BEST OF TIMES, INC.
147 Corporate Way
Birmingham, Alabama 35124
(205) 663-7248

Family photograph albums are a Southern tradition. The photographs
in this book came from the albums of Nash Presley Pritchett, Elvis'
aunt, and his cousins Donna Presley Early and Edie Hand.

Jacket Design by Robert Aulicino
Art Direction by Steve Parker
Production by Hand Made Books

Printed in the United States of America

1st Printing, 1997

ISBN 1-886049-10-6
Library of Congress Catalog Card Number Pending

Distributed by Southern Publishers Group
1-800-628-0903

To the fans of Elvis Presley around the world. It is to you that we dedicate *Elvis: Precious Memories,* so that you may know and remember him forevermore as we do — with loving, precious memories.

Acknowledgments

We cannot begin to express our appreciation to Susie Pritchett for her help in making this book possible. Her input was invaluable. Our heartfelt thanks and love to Buddy Early and Linc Hand for their assistance and support in addition to the family and friends who helped with our labor of love toward this project. Without their assistance *Elvis: Precious Memories* would not be a reality.

Our special thanks to Nash Presley Pritchett, known to us as "Mama" and "Aunt Nash," for leaving us so many precious memories of our family and especially the ones of Elvis.

—Donna Presley Early
—Edie Hand

I want to express my appreciation to the following people for their assistance in the research on and preparation of this book: Ottie Akers, Betty Caldwell, Shasta Edge, Susann Hamlin, Melanie Knight, Carolyn Laird, Barbara Parker, Garland Reeves, Nancy and Joe Ruzicka Rubye Sisson, and Anita Smith.

I especially would like to thank Judy Hunnicutt. Her joy in this project has kept me going.

—Lynn Edge

Contents

Contents

Foreword

I AM GLAD TO see that a book about Elvis has been written by these members of the Presley family, Donna Presley Early and Edie Hand. They have the ability to reveal an inside view that perhaps has not been seen before.

It was my privilege to know Elvis throughout his adult life — from the days he was in Sunday School at First Assembly of God in south Memphis until his death.

Many times after we attended services at First Assembly, Elvis and a group of us would go to nearby East Trigg Baptist Church to listen to the choir. East Trigg was the home church of many fine black gospel singers. The pastor at that time was Rev. Herbert Brewster, who was the author of a number of great gospel songs.

The choir's music was broadcast live over WHBQ, but we were fortunate enough to be there in person to hear them sing. It was something we really enjoyed. I believe this experience had a real influence on Elvis and helped underscore the lasting love he had for gospel music.

When Elvis' mother died, the Blackwood Brothers were asked to sing at her funeral. I remember that Elvis went over to his mother's casket, leaned over and kissed her and said,

"Mama, I would give every dime I have to have you back."
I was deeply moved by his display of devotion.

I got a call from Elvis when he came home from the Army.
He said, "The first night the quartet has off from your concert schedule, come out and let's sing together. I haven't got
ten to sing with anyone in so long." We went over to
Graceland and sang gospel songs around the piano for hours.

The picture in this book of Elvis, J.D. Sumner, Hovie
Lister and me was made at the Ellis Auditorium as the four
of us were singing "How Great Thou Art" backstage during
a gospel quartet convention. I want to reunite that quartet
in Heaven someday so we can sing that song together again.

The last time I heard Elvis sing "How Great Thou Art"
was at the Tarrant County Coliseum in Fort Worth, Texas.
As I was visiting with him later that night, I told him how
much I enjoyed his singing that song. A few years later, at
the request of his family, I sang that song at Elvis' funeral.

I invite you to read and enjoy this book written by Donna
Presley Early and Edie Hand with Lynn Edge.

—James Blackwood

Introduction

PEOPLE HAVE ASKED US why, almost 20 years after Elvis' death, we've decided to write a book about him. The answer is simple — Nashval Presley Pritchett. She was both the catalyst for this book and the reason it couldn't be written sooner.

Nash, Elvis' aunt and an Assembly of God minister, always wanted the world to know the Elvis Aaron Presley that his family knew and loved. The world has seen Elvis as the superstar, the talented, sensuous and handsome man who thrilled millions with his singing talent. His family knew him as a warm, funny, loving, compassionate and intelligent individual who had a strong faith in God.

We did not write this book because we think the world needs another book about Elvis. There have been plenty of books written about him. But those books did not show the public the side of Elvis that his family knew. Nash always wanted to write a book that would tell people the story of the Presley family, how we affected Elvis and how he affected us. She died before she had the opportunity to bring that book to the public.

Now we, her daughter and her cousin, want to tell that story for her. We want to talk about Elvis and our lives with him. We want to show how he was a positive influence on our lives.

—Donna Presley Early
—Edie Hand

The most disturbing part of this book deals with Elvis' death. It is a story Nash made me promise never to tell. When mom died, I felt I was released from that promise, and I am ready for the world to know what the family believes happened on that day at Graceland.

Writing this book has taken me on a painful journey through Elvis' autopsy report and the events of the day he died. It has, however, brought me to a peace in knowing more about what happened and coming to terms with why he is gone.

—Donna Presley Early

I want to dedicate this book to Elvis and Nash's memories and the legacy of never-ending love and true family values they left behind. This book is also dedicated to the memory of my special grandmother, Alice Hood Hacker, and to David and Phillip Blackburn, my precious brothers, who have all gone to be with the Lord.

—Edie Hand

A Note to the Reader

THIS IS A "FAMILY BOOK."

It is written as a collection of warm, personal memories revealed to you, the reader, by members of Elvis Presley's family.

The purpose of this book is to give you deep insight into Elvis Presley himself and into members of Elvis' family.

In keeping with the personal tone of this book, we often use only first names when quoting people or when we refer to them. We even have extended this first-name policy to two of the co-authors of the book, Donna Presley Early and Edie Hand. When you meet them in the book, they simply will be "Donna" and "Edie."

It seemed a natural way to refer to people in Elvis' life. As you read the book, the key figures will be sharing such intimate details with you that we hope you will feel you know them well enough to be on a first-name basis. For, after all, they are "family."

To help you get acquainted with these people, here is a look at some of them:

Donna—Donna Kay Presley Early. One of the co-authors of this book, she is Elvis' first cousin. Her mother, Nash, was the youngest sister of Elvis' father, Vernon. While growing up, Donna spent her summers at Graceland. After Elvis' death, she worked at Graceland.

Edie—Edith Mae Blackburn Hand. Another co-author and Elvis' cousin, Edie visited Graceland often. Edie's maternal grandmother, Alice Hacker, was the niece of Minnie Mae Presley (Elvis' paternal grandmother).

*Nash—Nashval Presley Pritchett. Elvis' aunt, the youngest sister of Elvis' father, Vernon, Nash was nine years old when Elvis was born. She lived near Elvis in Tupelo and helped to babysit him when he was young. She and Elvis were close during childhood and after they became adults. At one time, she and her family lived in a mobile home on the Graceland property directly behind the mansion. Nash completed her memoirs about Elvis several years before her death in 1994. Now, in this book, excerpts from those memoirs come alive for the first time for a national and international audience.

Vernon—Vernon Elvis Presley. Elvis' father and the son of Minnie Mae and Jesse D. Presley. Except for one period when he had a home near Graceland, he lived in his son's home from the time Elvis purchased Graceland. Not only was he Elvis' father, but he was one of the singer's most trusted advisors.

Gladys—Gladys Love Smith Presley. Elvis' mother and the sister of Clettus Smith, who married Elvis' uncle Vester Presley. Gladys lived in Graceland with her son and husband for a short while before her death. (Elvis also had an Aunt Gladys, his father Vernon's sister.)

Minnie—Minnie Mae Presley. Minnie was Elvis' paternal grandmother and the mother of Vernon Presley, Vester

Presley, Nash Presley Pritchett, Delta Presley Biggs and Gladys Presley Dowling. She lived at Graceland with Elvis and other members of his family. Elvis and some members of his family called Minnie "Dodger." Donna also called her "Grandma." You will find her referred to all three ways in this book. There also may be some confusion about the spelling of Minnie's middle name. On her birth certificate, it is spelled "May." She began a family tradition, however, by changing that spelling to "Mae." Except where official documents are concerned, her name is spelled "Mae" in this book.

Jesse—Jesse Presley. Elvis' grandfather and Dodger's husband. Elvis' twin, Jessie, was named for Jesse, though no family member seems to be able to account for the differences in the spelling of the two names.

Priscilla—Priscilla Beaulieu Presley. Elvis' wife and the mother of Lisa Marie Presley.

Lisa Marie—Lisa Marie Presley. Elvis' only child.

Delta—Delta Presley Biggs. Elvis' aunt, the daughter of Minnie Mae and Jesse D. Presley. Delta lived and worked at Graceland after the death of her husband.

Vester—Vester Presley. Elvis' uncle, Vester is the brother of Vernon Presley and the son of Minnie Mae and Jesse D. Presley. Vester married Clettus Smith, the sister of Vernon's wife, Gladys. He was an employee at Graceland for many years and still visits there every day.

Clettus—Clettus Smith Presley. Vester's wife and Gladys Love Smith Presley's sister.

Patsy—Patsy Presley. The daughter of Vester and Clettus Presley, Patsy is Elvis' double first cousin. She worked in Vernon's office at Graceland for a number of years.

Susie—Karen Sue Pritchett. The daughter of Earl and Nash Pritchett, she is Elvis' first cousin. Susie, Donna's sister, spent a great deal of time at Graceland when she was growing up and, after Elvis' death, she worked there.

Earl—Earl Pritchett. Nash's husband and the father of Donna and Susie. He lived in a mobile home on the Graceland grounds with his wife and family. He was an employee at Graceland for more than 20 years.

Buddy—Buddy Early. Donna Presley Early's husband. He was a security guard at Graceland after Elvis' death.

Dee—Dee Stanley Presley. Vernon Presley's second wife and Elvis' stepmother. Vernon met Dee while he was living in Germany during Elvis' tour of duty there. She and Vernon were divorced in 1977.

Sandy—Sandy Miller. Sandy came to work as Vernon's nurse, but their relationship grew beyond that and, at the time of Vernon's death, Sandy was his fiancee.

*All indented, italicized material in this book was taken from the memoirs of Nash Presley Pritchett.

Elvis: Precious Memories

"Prayer was and always has been an important part of life for the Presley family."

BEING A CLOSE FAMILY has made the Presleys a family of worriers. They worry about things like whether they've changed the batteries in the smoke alarm and whether or not their children — even the grown ones — have gotten home safely each day.

Given this family history, it should come as no surprise to learn that there were people in the family worrying about Elvis Aaron Presley even before he was born. Nashval Lorene Presley, Vernon's baby sister and Elvis' aunt, was only nine years old when Elvis was born.

She was just the right age for being curious about where babies come from and for listening when the grown-ups were talking. She overheard a lot. She recalled:

> After Vernon and Gladys got married, they lived with us for a while. Then, Vernon, Daddy and Vester (Vernon's brother) built the little house they lived in when the twins were born. There was a little friction between my dad and Gladys at times. Nothing serious, though. My mom could get along with anyone, though. And she and Gladys had a good relationship.

Mom and Dad were so happy when they found out they were going to be grandparents. And I couldn't wait to have a little baby to play with. And...I really was excited about being able to take care of a new little member of our family...

A few days before the twins were born, I heard Mom say to Daddy that she was worried about Gladys and that she hoped she wouldn't have a hard delivery.

Dad said, "Ah, she's a strong girl and she will be okay."

And Mom replied with, "But Vernon said she hasn't been feeling too good."

When the day arrived for the twins to be born, Vernon came over to our house to get Mom to be there with them and help the doctor. But that wasn't anything new to Mom. She always helped the neighbors when there was a new baby in the family or if there was a death in the family. She always tended to her own business and stayed at home. But if she was needed, she was there.

Mom was irritated the day the twins were born. She didn't think the doctor was doing all he could for Gladys, especially after they found there were twins. I'm sure the doctor was doing everything in his power, but when it's your loved ones, I think anyone would feel it wasn't enough.

When the twins were born, one was named Elvis Aaron, for their father, Vernon Elvis, and for Aaron Kennedy, one of Gladys and Vernon's best friends. The other was given the name Jessie Garon for Vernon's father, Jesse.

Nash (what everyone in the family called Nashval) soon found out that there was a sad side to the day she had looked forward to for so long. Jessie Garon was stillborn. She talked about that day:

Vernon and Gladys were heartbroken over the loss

of one child and yet so thankful to our God that the other baby was spared. Although one child could never take the place of another in our family, Vernon and Gladys were so elated that they would have a chance to bring this one that was left into their hearts and blend their love together in their small home and share their joy in the rearing of the tiny bundle lying on their bed.

And so January 8, 1935, ended — a day full of emotions for the Presley family. A new baby, but also a death in the family. And another thing to worry about.

"I remember Mom saying," Nash recalled, 'We almost lost Gladys.' "

Speaking of Gladys — much has been said over the years about Elvis' relationship with his mother. A lot of people try to make it an almost unnatural relationship, one that borders on incest. That's just not true. To really understand the relationship they had, you have to understand the time and the place where Elvis was born and the family into which he was born.

1935 wasn't a particularly great year anywhere in America. The whole country was suffering through the Great Depression. It wasn't a "three-bedroom, three-bath" time in America. Most people considered themselves lucky to have a home of any kind and having the luxury of giving each family member his own bedroom was practically unheard of. It certainly wasn't the norm in Tupelo, Mississippi.

All over the nation every night, children shared their parents' bedroom. It wasn't anything odd or perverted. It was a fact of life during the Depression. You were just lucky if it was only your immediate family that was sharing the house — and the bedroom.

Usually there were cousins, grandparents, aunts and uncles scattered all over the place — the little ones sleeping together on pallets, the grown-ups squeezing more than one bed into what usually was the only bedroom and getting by while they waited for better times.

It also wasn't a time in America when women worked outside their homes. Their homes, their families were their jobs. The men were the breadwinners. The women were the homemakers. It was as simple as that.

Men were responsible for seeing to it that there was a roof over the family's head and food on the table. Women were responsible for seeing that the house was kept neat and clean, the children were well cared for and the food was cooked. It was, for the times, a simple and practical division of labor.

To be a successful wife and mother was the same as being a brilliant scientist or a wealthy banker. It meant you had done your job well. Gladys Presley started out with one strike against her in this pursuit to do her job well. One of her children was dead.

It might not make sense in light of today's knowledge and mores, but that was something of a failure in those times. It meant she hadn't been able to protect that child from whatever kept him from living.

And it seemed to double her determination to see to it that her remaining child was going to be taken care of properly. If it meant that she practically never took her eye off him, if it meant that he was regarded by other people as a "Momma's Boy," it didn't really matter. Gladys Presley was going to care for her son. She wasn't going to fail again at taking care of her little family.

And it formed a bond between Elvis and his mother that was stronger than many people could understand. Gladys and Elvis had been a team since the day Elvis was born. It was a team that both of them seemed to think would go on forever. Together they would face the world, together they would overcome it. They would be each other's shield and each other's strength.

And when the unthinkable happened and Elvis lost his mother, it brought about a change in him that never went away.

Of course, Gladys' worrying wasn't limited to Elvis. Vester, who had dated Gladys before she and Vernon met and who eventually married her sister, Clettus, recalls that "Gladys worried about Clettus that way, too. And others in the family. It was just her nature."

People have said that Elvis wasn't close to his father. That's not true. Again, Elvis was very much a product of the time and place in which he grew up. The South always has been a very matriarchal society. Men are the head of the family, but women are the head of the house and there's an important difference there. The term "Steel Magnolias" isn't just a movie title. It's the real thing.

It may be less that way today than it was when Elvis was growing up, but you'll still find your share of those Steel Magnolias scattered all over the South.

Still, even though the mother was expected to pretty much run the household, including the kids, children had a relationship with their fathers. It wasn't any less close than with their mothers, it was just different.

Their fathers were their protectors, their providers. Boys learned how men took care of their families by watching their fathers. And they learned to appreciate what they had when they saw how tired their fathers came in at night after a full day's work.

Elvis was no different. He saw how hard his father worked to take care of him and his mother. He saw his uncles work to care for their families. And he came to accept the fact that he was in charge of protecting and caring for his mother when his father was working. He and Vernon shared that special appreciation, respect and love for one another that most Southern men had instilled in them from the minute they could toddle around the house. You might not see them hugging one another, but you could tell when they were together exactly how they felt about each other.

To really understand Elvis you have to understand how a Southern family of the 1930s worked. Families then usually were large. The more children the family had, the more built-in field hands they had. If you didn't have enough children to help you get your crop in, you had to hire someone and that meant less money for you.

Often, your wife would join you in the field or in the barn or wherever you were working. What happened to the children while the two of you were trying to force a living from the land was that the ones not old enough to be out there working were at home, looking after the little ones.

Just because of the natural progression of things, each child — particularly the girls — had a younger brother or sister that was his or her responsibility. It wasn't necessarily a bad way to grow up. The girls were going to grow up to be wives and mothers and they got plenty of practice while they were young. Having that child to care for was sort of a badge of honor. It was sort of the '30s equivalent of every little girl having a Cabbage Patch doll. Everybody else had one, so naturally you wanted one, too.

What was frustrating for Nash, of course, was that, since she was the youngest of Jesse and Minnie's children, she didn't have a baby to care for. And that's why she latched on to Elvis for all she was worth. He was her chance to play momma for a while.

In the days before the twins were born, she thought about what it was going to be like having a little one follow her around, taking every step she took. She couldn't wait.

Gladys, set from the beginning of Elvis' life in her role as a protective mother, had a hard time letting Nash step into the role for which she felt she was destined. But she finally felt confident enough that Elvis wasn't going to break that she began to let Nash hold him. At least once, however, Gladys had reason to think she might have been right about never turning him over to anyone else. Nash recalled one exciting event from Elvis' infancy:

> *As Elvis began to get a little older, Gladys and Vernon would let me hold him. One day, I was rocking him in front of the fireplace and Gladys came in to take him from me so she could give him a bath. I stood up to hand Elvis to her and dropped him, but just before he hit the hearth, I reached out and grabbed him by the diaper. Thank the Lord for cloth diapers*

back then. Somehow, I don't think the popular brands most mothers use now would have held together.

Despite that near-miss, Gladys continued to let Nash care for Elvis. Nash continued:

> *When Elvis started walking, I was allowed to take him out in the yard. I would show him different things to see how he would pronounce their different names. I would call them by their names and ask him to repeat after me.*
>
> *He would try and it was so cute the way he called things. Elvis always called animals and people by unusual names.*

Water, for some reason, was "duckling" to the young Elvis. Like most, Elvis' family didn't try to find out why he used the wrong names for things, they just figured out what he meant and went on. If he wanted to call water "duckling" and that was the most they ever had to figure out about him, so be it.

One of Elvis' mispronunciations has become a thing of legend. There are all sorts of stories about how his grandmother Minnie got her nickname — "Dodger." All the stories agree that it came from Elvis, but, beyond that fact, the variations are many. Actually, according to Donna, it simply sprang from the fact that when Elvis was young, he couldn't say "Grandmother," pronouncing it "Granddodger" instead. Over the years, he shortened it to "Dodger," the name he and a chosen few were allowed to call Minnie Mae.

One didn't sit down for eight–course meals during the Depression in America, but parents did want their children to eat what was put before them. Elvis' family was no exception. And Elvis, like most children growing up in the South at the time, thought that the food at Grandmother's house was the best. Nash said:

> *He liked to eat at our house and always wanted*

*to eat out of the same dishes. So Mom would wash
his dishes and put them up in the china cabinet in one
corner by themselves.*

Despite all of Minnie's and Gladys' best efforts to see
that the youngster ate all the right things, Grandmother's
cooking wasn't the only food Elvis got served when he went
over to his grandparents' house. Once again, he was bound
to have an adventure and once again, it was thanks to Nash.
She told this story about introducing a new item to his menu:

*Our house sat a little high off the ground and my
friends and I would get under there and build sand
castles and make mud pies. As Elvis got a little older,
he wanted to play in the sand and build sand castles
and make mud pies, too...One time, I asked Elvis to
taste a mud pie I had made. He did and about that
time, Gladys came out to get him for lunch.*

*She said, "Elvis, come out and eat your lunch,"
to which he replied "I've already eaten." She said,
"Did Grandma fix your lunch?" He said, "No, Aunt
Nash made a pie and I ate a piece of it and I'm not
hungry."*

*Gladys said, "You two get out here this minute!"
(He had mud all over his mouth and he didn't want
Gladys to see it.) She took one look at his little mouth
with mud all over it and shook her finger at me and
said, "Young lady, you knew better than that and it
had better never happen again!"...I promise you, it
didn't.*

The older and more mobile Elvis got, the more "adven-
tures" he and Nash could have. And the more Gladys found
herself wondering if her son would make it through what
was, after all, just a normal childhood.

Once when Nash was trying to help him learn to ride a
bicycle, she was holding him up on the bike and he fell off.
She recalled what happened next:

Gladys came running out there and said, "You've killed my baby!" Now, Elvis only got a few bruises but I was scared out of a year's growth.

Nash threw more than a few scares into Gladys and when Gladys scolded her for a misadventure she and Elvis had undertaken, Gladys could throw a scare into Nash. At least one time, however, Gladys scared Nash when she didn't mean to. Nash told the story this way:

Sometimes Elvis and I would go up behind the house and play in the pasture. One day, we were up there playing and Gladys called out to us that there was a cow in the pasture. She only wanted us to know that the cow was there so we could watch her, but I thought she said the cow was after us.

So I picked Elvis up and ran as fast as I could until I got through the gate and up to the porch. Gladys was standing there laughing so hard, with tears streaming down her face.

I want you to know that I didn't appreciate it one bit, because I failed to see the humor in it. I thought I had probably saved Elvis' life and it had taken all the energy I could muster up just to carry him.

Gladys worried about who was watching Elvis, but that was something over which she did have some control. Gladys' worrying also extended to things she couldn't do a thing about except panic. Nash said:

Gladys had an unusual fear of storms and when a cloud came up, she and Mom would take us to the storm cellar. I didn't like to go into the storm cellar. I would just as soon have taken my chances with a storm as with the snakes that could have been in that cellar.

If a storm came up and Gladys couldn't make it to the cellar, she would take Elvis and get under the bed.

> *One time, the doctor was there to see Elvis and*
> *a storm came up. So Gladys picked up Elvis and went*
> *to the storm cellar, just leaving the good doctor back*
> *at the house.*

Nash probably did a lot to instill a sense of adventure in Elvis. That was one of the by-products of having the older children sort of raise the younger ones. Children are more willing to step out on faith and not stop to think about what the consequences of their actions might be.

They see a tool shed with a tin roof and, most likely, they are going to see if they can fashion themselves some wings to fly off of it. They don't calculate the risk of cuts from rusty tin or broken bones from crash landings. For children, there aren't many things that aren't possible. And if it looks like fun, they are willing to give it a try.

Elvis might have had fewer bruises if he hadn't spent so much childhood time with his Aunt Nash, but he might not have known how to ride a bicycle either.

Another thing he might have gotten from Nash was a trait that lasted a lifetime — a love of fine automobiles.

The first ones he had might not have been fine in the Henry Ford sense of the word, but they were fine by childhood standards. And you might say that Elvis' first car was a "Nash." (That is, if you consider a car built by Nashval Lorene Presley a "Nash.") His aunt talked about building those vehicles:

> *I used to build cars for us and we would pull them*
> *out onto the driveway and pretend we were*
> *driving...the steering wheels were made out of lids*
> *off of two lard buckets and the floorboards were from*
> *pieces of rough lumber, but we got many miles out of*
> *those old cars...*

After Elvis became a star, he often presented family members and friends with cars as gifts. But as Nash pointed out, their childhood was "the only time my car ever looked as good as his. Maybe it was because I built them."

Another thing that Elvis learned from Nash — and the rest of his family — was a love of music. Nash remembered:

> I used to take Elvis out on the front porch of their little house and hold him in the swing and sing to him. I didn't know it at the time, but one day he would sing not only to me, but to the entire world.
>
> We all liked music and we loved to sing. We had an organ and guitars. Sometimes we would sit around in the living room and play and sing.
>
> Vernon would usually just sing. He liked the song "Corrina! Corrina!" It was easy to play so we sang that one quite often. Sometimes Vernon and Gladys would dance and sometimes Vester and Clettus would dance to a waltz tune.
>
> I watched Vester play the chords and I would make the same chords he did. That's the way I learned to play guitar.
>
> Sometimes Vernon and Gladys would sing together in church. There were times Elvis sang with them.

The grown-up Elvis loved flowers, especially roses. It was a love he acquired early on. Nash remembered what joy he took in picking flowers for his mother and his grandmother. Nash told how Elvis started giving the gift of flowers:

> My mind drifts back to our childhood days and I still can see a little Southern boy reaching up to grab Morning Glory blossoms from a vine my Mom had running up on heavy string to shade the porch from the sun. He would grab a little fistful and run to his mom, Gladys, and my mom and stand there with his little face beaming, waiting to see if they would take him in their arms, hug him and tell him they loved him for being so thoughtful to bring them the pretty blue blossoms.

*Although there weren't enough (flowers) to put
in a vase, he would wait to see if they were going to
put them in water and, of course, they did.*

Church was another thing that Elvis was introduced to
early in his life. As was customary at that time in America,
church was not only the place where you went for spiritual
renewal. It was a social center as well.

You worked hard all week long and on the Sabbath, you
rested. You went with your family and friends to whatever
church you had chosen. That visit to church meant you got
to see your neighbors and ask after the health of their family
members. The men talked about the weather and the crops.
The women talked about new marriages, new babies and
deaths.

Probably the majority of marriages were sort of "made
in Heaven" at that time because church was usually where
you met the person you were going to marry. Many a preacher
stood at the front of a church to marry second, third and
even fourth generations of families.

And babies who came into those families were at church
just as regularly as their parents. At that time, there weren't
church nurseries or "cry rooms." Sermons often were punc-
tuated by the fussing of a little one, and more than one youngster got a stern admonition to sit still and listen during
"preaching."

So it wasn't a bit surprising to see Vernon, Gladys and
Elvis take their places in the pew on Sunday at the Assembly
of God church the Presley family attended. Nash said:

*Prayer was and always has been an important part
of life for the Presley family. I can remember Vernon
on his knees in church praying. I heard him so many
times in his bedroom praying when Elvis was small.*

*Elvis would lay his hands on Vernon and Gladys
when they were sick and pray for them. He would
tell them, "Jesus will make it all better."*

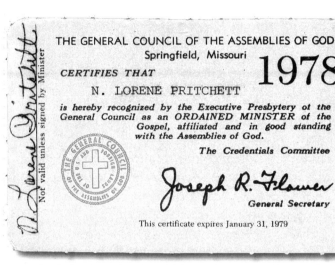

Assemblies of God membership card for Nash Lorene Prichett, verifying she was an ordained minister.

Praying was — and still is — just a part of life for people in the Presley family. You learned to "talk to God" when you were small and you just kept on doing it the rest of your life. Of course, not every member of the family kept up that prayer with the same consistency. For some, it has been as much a part of their lives as breathing. For others, it is a source of strength when things aren't going well.

No one who knew him well questions that Elvis was intelligent. That intelligence coupled with his early exposure to church led him to a curiosity about God and the Bible and religion — all types of religion —that went with him throughout his life.

He read voraciously and, often, he was reading about the Bible or about religion. Even after he was grown, he and Nash would discuss the meaning of scriptures and other aspects of religion for hours on end.

Elvis was introduced to religion when he still was very young, but that doesn't mean he spent his childhood as a saint. The fact is — and some people surely will disagree on this one — boys are boys and girls are girls and raising one isn't like raising the other.

A little girl will look at a clock and wonder what time it is. A little boy looks at one and wonders how many screws he'll have to take out to get it apart. Little girls generally pick quieter, more sedate games. Little boys' games involve running and making noise.

Which probably is why Nash had the experience she did when, as a child, she was playing "church teacher." Nash remembered the story this way:

One thing I liked to do was go down to the Methodist church in front of our house, stick sticks up in the ground and pretend I was teaching. My friend and I would take turns with teaching at times and some times I would go out there with Elvis and I would preach to the sticks.

I must say they were a pretty good congregation. They never complained about my sermons. But I couldn't get anyone to feel convicted enough to go to the altar.

...it didn't help a bit when Elvis would pull my congregation up and throw them. I guess it's a little hard to be spiritual while you are flying through the air and it wasn't the Holy Spirit that sent you flying.

2

"He said he was going to buy his mom and dad a big house and many cars."

THE DESIRE TO MAKE music was something that was inborn in Elvis Presley. It was part of the Presley DNA, passed along from generation to generation as surely as the color of hair and eyes, as much a part of a Presley's being as the shape of the family nose or chin.

When Elvis was small, he had a toy guitar, according to their neighbors the Kennedys and would stand on the porch and serenade them, pretending to play.

Edie recalls that Elvis once told her that when he was young, he thought he had a calling to sing gospel music. "He was programmed to that. His first singing was in the church," she says. Even though that wasn't the direction his singing career took, it was a love he never lost. When he was just sitting around the piano at Graceland, singing with the family, it usually was a gospel song that his fingers would seek out. If there could be such a thing as a "gospel music gene," you'd find it on all the Presley chromosomes.

There have been many stories about how Elvis got his first real guitar. The one you hear the most is that Gladys bought it for him. She got him the guitar, the story goes, because what he really wanted was a bicycle and she was afraid he would get hurt on one. The guitar was to take the place of the bicycle.

Of course, that doesn't make much sense when you know that Nash taught Elvis to ride a bicycle. Gladys apparently already had faced that fear and overcome it — or at least learned to deal with it.

Donna thinks that his Uncle Vester first put Elvis in touch with the guitar. "Vester probably thought maybe the family could use another band member and he gave Elvis a guitar. It probably was just an old one that he had and didn't play anymore," she says. (Later, Elvis' father bought him a guitar — one Elvis appreciated even more due to the fact that he knew his family couldn't afford it and that it had been a sacrifice for them to buy it for him.) According to Nash, the family always was sitting around singing and making music and the thought that some family member would just pass an old instrument on to a younger member makes a lot of sense, especially when you remember that this wasn't a family with a lot of extra money to spend on things such as guitars.

The thing is, it really doesn't matter how Elvis got his first guitar. The fact is that, somehow, he did get one. And he learned to play it.

There might have been times when Elvis was growing up that he picked up that guitar, strummed it and pretended he was on stage in front of an auditorium full of rapt listeners. Or he might have imagined that he was at the Grand Ole Opry, playing and singing with the country music greats. Even a child from the poorest part of Tupelo, Mississippi, has dreams. He may not believe in his heart of hearts that they will come true, but he has dreams.

Elvis had some down-to-earth plans for his life, according to Nash. She and Elvis spent a lot of "front porch time" talking about their futures. Nash said:

> *We talked about what we would like to be when we grew up. He said he wanted to be a truck driver and a singer and I said I would like to be a nurse and*

*a gospel singer...one of those dreamers became a pretty
popular singer and it wasn't me.*

*...he said he was going to buy his mom and dad a
big house and many cars. And as you know, that
dream came true.*

Gladys probably saw her son getting a job as a truck
driver or doing some kind of job that involved working with
his hands. In truth, as most people who know Elvis' story
are aware, he was a truck driver for a while. But Donna says
that Elvis "always had this feeling. He always saw himself in
a bigger situation than being in Tupelo."

Even though Gladys probably would have liked to think
of Elvis using his musical talents to become a big star, she
most likely filed that idea away in the "wouldn't it be nice"
category. Being poor has a way of making you dream big
dreams and a way of imposing reality on those dreams every
day.

Elvis' face would become one of the most photographed
in the world, but the young Elvis didn't like getting his picture made at all. One image of him that everyone has seen is
one where he's standing between his mother and his father.
Elvis, very young at the time, is wearing overalls and a hat
set at an angle. His mouth is held in a crooked, pensive half-
smile. Many people have speculated that this was the beginning of the famous "lip twitch" with which Elvis would tease
his audiences in later years. In reality, it's the result of a bribe.

Elvis loved peanuts. On this day, Vernon and Gladys told
him if he would be still and get his picture made, he could
have a peanut. He has it in his mouth in the picture.

Elvis' family always knew he was an intelligent child.
But that's another thing about growing up in the South. Even
if you know your child is the most exceptional ever, you
don't go around bragging about it. Oh sure, you might mention to your friends and family if he happens to get "straight
A's" on his report card, but you don't go around talking
about how you're sure he's a candidate for a Nobel Prize.
You wait for someone else to say it. If the child is as smart as

you think, someone else will notice and that person — usually a teacher — will mention it to you when you go to the annual PTA Open House. That's how it was done in the South when Elvis was a child. And if your child was the very best academically or even if he wasn't, you wanted him to be well-behaved and polite. It was expected of children then. Teachers noticed that, too. And you'd find out how your offspring was doing behavior-wise — one way or the other. If he was causing trouble, you'd usually get a note from the teacher. If he was doing well, she'd mention that at the PTA meeting as well.

Elvis was doing very well in that regard. Oleta Grimes, his fifth-grade teacher at Tupelo's Lawhorn Elementary School, once said she remembered Elvis as a real good little boy who liked people and knew God.

It was in Mrs. Grimes' class that Elvis premiered his monumental talent for his schoolmates. Each morning when it was time for the little chapel service Mrs. Grimes conducted to start the day, Elvis would be the first to volunteer to sing a solo.

Mrs. Grimes taught all of her classes a song called "Old Shep." When Elvis learned it, he played guitar and sang it for the rest of her class. Mrs. Grimes even called the principal down to listen to Elvis sing. That's when she and the principal decided to sponsor him in the Mississippi-Alabama Fair in Tupelo. Elvis won second place at that fair. First place went to a six-year-old girl named Becky who sang "Sentimental Journey."

Elvis later remembered that day at the fair less for the fact that his singing won him a second place award and more for the fact that his mother spanked him for something the same day.

In 1952, Elvis went to sing at the Jimmie Rodgers Day Show, a forum for untried singers in Meridian. He was 17 years old and scared to death. Before he stepped up to the microphone, he ran his fingers nervously across his guitar. He turned to the emcee and asked, "Sir, can they hear me in Tupelo?"

The emcee smiled and assured him that everything was going to be fine, that he should just do his best and "get in there and sing." Elvis was shaking so hard he almost couldn't make it to the microphone, so the emcee gave him an encouraging shove and Elvis began his song.

After the show was over, Elvis told the emcee, Roger Thames, that it was the first time he had ever been anywhere or done anything outside his hometown of Tupelo.

Basically, Elvis lived the life of a typical Southern youth of the 1940s. He went to school, he went to church, he remembered to say, "Yes, ma'am" and "No, sir" and he moved when his family moved. Which is how he, Vernon, Gladys and various Presley relatives ended up in Memphis.

In Memphis, Elvis and his family started out living in the Lauderdale Courts Housing Project. One former resident of those projects recalled that Elvis was sweet, not stupid. Elvis was nice, too, one of the nicest kids in the projects. It's a fact of life, there always are going to be rough kids who seek out the ones who are nice and try — through intimidation and more than a few brawls — to toughen them up. Around Lauderdale Courts, those kids stuck Elvis with two nicknames. He was "Little Lord Fauntleroy" or "Hillbilly."

On a January morning not long after the Presleys moved to Memphis, Elvis and his mother were walking down the sidewalk toward Humes High School when the neighborhood kids spotted him. What made Elvis, who would be the new kid at school, so noticeable was that, even though he was a teenager, his mother was walking him to school.

He walked the entire distance to school holding Gladys' hand that morning. And when school was dismissed that afternoon, Gladys was waiting to walk her son home. Gladys, the neighbors whispered among themselves, was afraid of Memphis. She had heard too many reports about the kinds of things that went on in big cities like this one. And she was terrified for her son. Somehow, she believed that she could ward off harm if she was with him. Walking him to and from school was her ritual of protection. Years later, when Elvis got a job as an usher at a movie theater, Gladys walked her son to work.

Elvis could have friends in the projects and at school, but they had to pass Gladys' inspection.

One project resident, a young lady, thought of Elvis as a nice enough person, but a real mama's boy. Even when he was a teenager, he had to ask his mother's permission just to go down the street with his friends and he had to let her know how long he thought they would be gone.

There are some advantages to having a mother who hovers. She doesn't want you to be totally friendless, so she's nice to the other kids and invites them over to your house so you won't ask if you can go to theirs. Gladys did that and it did somewhat make up for her inability to let him out of her sight. The Presley residence always was open to Elvis' friends and Gladys served as much iced tea, soft drinks and cake as they could consume. She doted on the youngsters and offered them advice.

One of Elvis' early girlfriends, one who apparently passed the Gladys test, dated Elvis for a number of years. When she would tell other people that she was dating someone named Elvis, they would laugh at his name.

One person who thought the name was rather unusual, but found it attached to a very polite young man, was a woman who is a Birmingham, Alabama, resident today. The woman, a native of Russia, found herself living in Memphis, Tennessee, with her husband and young child in 1954. A neighbor had a 16-year-old daughter named Darlene, who babysat with the woman's toddler. The two families also became friends because, in addition to being neighbors, they shared another interest. The woman's husband was a Shriner as was Darlene's father.

Each year, the Shriners in Memphis hosted a circus-type event. In 1954, Darlene agreed to run the hot dog stand at the circus. One day at the circus, Darlene kept telling her neighbor, "You've got to stay around. My boyfriend's coming by to help and I want you to meet him," the woman recalls.

"I asked her what the boy's name was and she said, 'Elvis Presley.' Then she just went on and on, saying, 'He's a singer and he just cut his first record. He's going to be real famous someday.'

"I just smiled and let her talk, because I thought, 'Every girl is high on her boyfriend.' Then the boy came and he just looked like an ordinary boy, except with his hair all slicked back. He was very nice, very polite. He helped sell the hot dogs there that day.

"After that, I didn't think too much about him. I had a young child and a life. He was a nice boy, but I didn't give him much more thought."

Not long after that, she and her family moved to Newfoundland, leaving Memphis and Darlene behind. On September 9, 1956, the woman was sitting in Canada, watching *The Ed Sullivan Show*, when the announcer said, "Elvis Presley."

"I looked up at the television and there was the boy," she remembers. "I called my husband in there and said, 'Look, it's Darlene's boyfriend!' "

One can only imagine how Elvis would have felt about that reference. He probably would have gotten a chuckle out of the fact that, while he was a hot new singing sensation to most of the people watching that night, to at least one he was "Darlene's boyfriend."

"Darlene broke up with Elvis," the young woman's former neighbor explains. "The next time I heard from her, she was married to somebody else and was expecting a baby of her own."

One thing that attracted Darlene and other girls to Elvis was the obvious — his looks. He was very handsome until the day that Gladys for some reason gave him a home permanent. When one girl laughed, Elvis got mad and had most of his hair shaved off. When she laughed about that, he got mad all over again.

Unfortunately, Elvis was more serious about this particular girl than she was about him. When she ended the relationship, she quickly learned that she shouldn't let her dates take her to the movie theater where Elvis worked. They were sure to be in for an evening of hard stares and constant inspection by one of the ushers.

Life in the projects often involved having to engage in fisticuffs, but Elvis didn't participate. Gladys had taught him never to fight. That meant, of course, that he was on the receiving end of the flying fists more than once. He wasn't a sissy because he played the rough and tumble sports of the projects with the best of them. He just walked away rather than fight. That was the way he had been raised. In Elvis' adulthood, everyone knows, that way of dealing with things changed.

The laundry room at the projects turned out to be Elvis' first music studio. Jesse Lee Denson, one of Elvis' friends, was a semi-professional musician and Gladys asked his mother if Jesse Lee would teach Elvis to play the guitar. Vernon went out and bought his son a "Gene Autry" signature guitar. Jesse, whom Elvis called "Lay" (because that's the way Lee sounds when you pronounce it with a Deep-South, East Tupelo accent), gave Elvis lessons in the laundry room, where the acoustics were great.

Elvis would sit out on the steps at night and play and sing for the folks sitting out there. He had a good voice. Everyone knew that. His guitar playing, however, sometimes got in the way. He would stop in mid-song and say, "I forgot the chord." Even after he learned the chords he would sometimes pretend to forget, to be cute and funny.

Elvis was shy and it was hard to get him to open up to anyone. When he did find another teenager to talk to, though, he talked a lot. It became apparent to some of his friends that there were just going to be times when Elvis needed to talk and he needed someone to listen without judging. It was a problem that would go with him throughout his life.

It also didn't escape the notice of his friends that Elvis was "different," wearing his hair long when everyone else had a flattop. When the other kids were wearing Levi's, Elvis was wearing what some friends suspected were the only two pairs of pants that he owned.

One pair of the gabardine pants was black with a white stripe down the side and the other pair was black with a pink stripe.

A lot has been written about Elvis' "style" in high school, wearing clothes that were different from those of the other students and styling his hair differently. Some people think it was because he was trying to create an image for himself, even before anybody knew who he was. More than likely, though, he was compensating for some things — he was new to the school, coming at a time when the other students had formed cliques that went all the way back to grammar school, and he was from a family that didn't have a lot of money. Often when children of this age don't really fit into the "in-crowd" at their schools, they find ways to make up for it. Some become bullies; others wear clothes the "in" kids would never think of wearing. It's almost as if they are saying, "I wouldn't be in your group if you asked me, I like to dress this way."

Whatever the reason, Elvis began to take on a look that would set him apart from the crowd for the rest of his life. His hair always would be one of the first things you'd see when you looked at him. His clothes would be a style all his own.

Elvis didn't belong to any particular group in high school, he sort of remained a loner. He was low–key and didn't take part in many school activities. In fact, Elvis probably didn't even go to the prom. He was in ROTC, however, and played touch football.

There was one thing that would have made Elvis stand out even if his hair and clothes had been just like everyone else's. That was his car. It was a 1940 or 1941 Lincoln coupe. Those cars that Nash built for Elvis earlier obviously made him always want wheels that made him noticeable in a crowd.

Even though Elvis didn't do outlandish things that drew attention to himself, there was one thing that one friend, William Leaptrott, never forgot — the time Elvis played the guitar and sang a country song for the male beauty pageant at Humes High.

Despite the fact that he may not have fit in as well as some of the other 201 students in his graduating class, Elvis did make friends in high school. Some of them were friends that would be there until the day he died. In fact, his path crossed that of one of his classmates a lot after they graduated from high school. This fellow had become a photographer for a Memphis newspaper and often Elvis would let his friend make a photograph of him when he had turned away requests from hordes of other photographers. That was just Elvis. He and this person had been classmates. Elvis didn't forget it. They came from the same part of Memphis. Just because Elvis might have moved to a different part of the city didn't mean he was going to try and erase the memory of where he had come from.

Elvis took school seriously enough to get passing grades, even if they weren't the kind that were going to put him on the honor roll. The day he graduated from high school, Elvis came down off the stage, diploma in hand, and said, "I got it!"

After Elvis graduated from Humes, he drove a truck for a while, just as he predicted he would. But he didn't forget that he also wanted to be a singer. That Presley family connection to music didn't just fade away the first time Elvis slid under the steering wheel of a Crown Electric vehicle.

There probably isn't an Elvis fan alive who hasn't heard the story about Elvis' first recording session. The story is that he went into Sun Records to record two songs for his mother's birthday. Then someone has said that this first recording session was after his mother's birthday had passed, so the record couldn't have been made for her.

Those particulars don't really matter. The fact is that he went to Sun Studios in Memphis and recorded two songs. Sam Phillips heard them (again, there are a number of stories as to how this came about) and, to use an entertainment cliche, a star was born.

Of course, Sam Phillips and Marion Keisker, who has been described as Phillips' right arm, certainly were midwives at that birth. Miss Keisker called Edwin Howard, the entertainment writer for *The Memphis Press-Scimitar*, on the morning of July 27, 1954. She asked if she could bring a "promising Sun artist" by to meet Howard.

Howard said she told him they would have to come in on the boy's lunch hour, because he still was driving a truck for Crown Electric Company. Howard told her to bring the boy on down and, shortly after noon, they got off the elevator on the fifth floor of *The Press-Scimitar*.

Elvis' looks made a big impression on a lot of people during his career, but this wasn't one of those times when he could get by on looks alone. He recently had gotten what had to be one of his worst haircuts ever. He looked a little like his locks had been cut by a lawn mower. Still, some of the things that would become Elvis' trademarks already were there — flattop, ducktail and sideburns.

At this interview, Elvis showed his inexperience in dealing with the press. He sat there shyly, answering only "Yes, sir" and "No, sir," letting Miss Keisker do the rest of the talking.

The next day, Howard wrote a column about his young visitor. It may have been the first time a newspaper really took note of what Elvis would be offering the music world.

He reported that Elvis Presley just had signed a contract with Sun Record Company of Memphis. Already, the songs that Elvis had recorded for Sun were getting a lot of play time on the Memphis radio stations, not an easy feat for a newcomer to accomplish, and Howard was impressed. He opined that this might just be the biggest hit that Sun had ever pressed.

Life is sort of funny. We're always told to look before we leap. And, sometimes, we think it would be nice to know before making a decision whether it is going to be a big, life-changing one or one that just means we don't get to the grocery store at the time we had planned to. On the other hand, sometimes if we knew how very much one decision or another was going to change our lives, we might be too scared to go through with it.

If Elvis could have seen into the future that day when he found his way into Sun Records and known how much things were going to change for him and for his family, he might have run as fast as he could in the other direction.

Elvis always had led something of a sheltered life. Living in Tupelo and later in Memphis, he was surrounded by family. There were aunts, uncles and cousins only a few steps away. If he needed company or someone to go exploring in the woods with, there always was someone available and willing to join the conversation or adventure.

All that was about to change, however. Sam Phillips had heard something in those first two recordings Elvis made that he knew was going to take this youngster a long way from driving a truck for a local electric company.

It was the mixing of the black and white sounds popular at that time into one sound that made Elvis different. Presley, one music critic said, picked up several things from black music. "One was an uninhibited delivery... The other is hard to grab hold of — that attitude Presley brings to a song. He gets right inside the words, makes you feel low down. If a song is happy, he can ride on top of that feeling too."

Elvis wasn't a blues singer, wasn't strictly rock and roll. He wasn't country, although there was a lot of country in his style. He was Elvis.

"I think Elvis had such an impact on people because he started in 1953, not long after the end of World War II," Donna says. "The country still was in transition. People were looking for something different and Elvis was like something they never had seen before. He was a cross between spiritual and rock. It was just the right time for it. It was a whole new culture appearing on the horizon."

Before long, Elvis was making recordings, he was making personal appearances, he was making movies. He was making money. He didn't have to get by with the car he had driven since he was in high school anymore. He could have a new one whenever he wanted it. He didn't lack for people around him either. People who wouldn't give him a second look in high school suddenly wanted everyone to know they were members of Elvis' graduating class.

There was something else about Elvis that was going to set him apart from the rest and Sam Phillips saw that from the start as well. Without even being aware of it, Elvis Presley sent out shock waves of sexual tension wherever he went. Elvis, who always was close to his mother and father, was the cause of many arguments between parents and children. Mothers and fathers forbade their children to have Elvis' records in the house. That swivel-hipped, sexy way he moved when he sang came through the black plastic. You could feel it as you listened to the recordings and it couldn't do anything but lead impressionable teenagers astray. Preachers stepped into pulpits across the United States and told young people to throw away their Elvis records before they did something that would damn their souls forever. They might as well have been preaching to sticks the way Nash used to do, because those youngsters weren't about to give up Elvis. In truth, probably very few of the teenagers swooning over Elvis from the start committed one of the seven deadly sins based on something they heard in Elvis' voice, but their interest in this up–and–coming singing sensation caused their parents and their ministers to lose a lot of sleep.

"I would have loved to have been older then, to see what the first of this new era was like," Donna said. "Youth had a culture all its own in Elvis and the era of Rock. It was separate from their parents, something they could call their own."

At first, Elvis was represented by Bob Neal. But he hadn't escaped the notice of a man who variously has been described as a Svengali, a charlatan, a shrewd businessman. Colonel Tom Parker, who came from a medicine–show type background, may not have known much about anything else, but he knew talent when he saw it. Elvis had that talent.

"When I first saw Elvis, he had a million dollars worth of talent," Parker liked to say. He wanted to see to it that Elvis had that million dollars and he wanted to be the agent who shared in that good fortune.

Parker worked first through Neal, then supplanted him and became Elvis' manager. It was a job he would have for the rest of Elvis' life. In November, 1955, Elvis reached an agreement with Parker and signed a contract with RCA records. Sun Records got $40,000 in exchange for all that was Elvis. It isn't a lot of money by today's standards. In

Elvis Aaron Presley, 35—Musician/Entertainer—Memphis, Tennessee.

The success of Elvis Aaron Presley is a phenomenon of the entertainment world. Elvis is one of the most well known and prolific entertainers in the Nation. Fifty-one of his single records have won Gold Record awards for sales of more than one million records. Fourteen of his albums have won Gold Album awards. Over 200 million of his recordings have been sold around the world. He has sung and acted in 32 major motion pictures. Elvis performs before sell out crowds wherever he appears.

Elvis began his professional career with the Louisiana Hayride. In late 1955 his record, "That's All Right Mama," brought him national attention. Four television appearances with Tommy and Jimmy Dorsey, one with Milton Berle and four with Ed Sullivan made him a national entertainment figure.

From the United States Jaycees program honoring Elvis as one of America's Ten Outstanding Young Men, in ceremonies January 9, 1971, Memphis, Tennessee.

Elvis' record breaking entry into the music industry resulted in the creation of the first Gold Album award in 1957 when, for the first time, an album sold more than one million copies. The award presented to him read: "First Album to Sell One Million Copies — One of the Greatest Achievements in this History of the Record Industry.—1957."

In 1969 he won three gold records and albums: "His Hand in Mine", "In The Ghetto", and "Elvis TV Special". His television special the same year, demonstrated his remarkable talent, tradition and flair that continues to capture the imagination of millions.

Elvis has won multiple honors from virtually every entertainment industry group. His singing has brought 17 Broadcast Music Awards for individual songs. Elvis possesses a talent which spans decades and continents. He is a favorite of music lovers of all ages in the United States and around the world.

Despite the fact that he has never been in the United Kingdom, he has been Great Britain's leading recording artist for 14 years. Even in nations as remote as South Africa, he is well known. During 1960 a total of 10 million of his records were sold in South Africa.

The *Guinness Book of World Records* reported that Elvis had sold by January, 1965, total global sales of over 110,000,000 discs. His current sales record is more than 200,000,000.

Throughout his career Elvis has been one of the most civic-minded residents of Memphis, Tennessee, where he has lived since early in his career. Unlike many entertainers, he has intentionally concealed many acts of philanthropy which might have brought him considerable publicity. His personal donations to charity—totaling more than half a million dollars over the last 10 years—have been made with little fanfare. His efforts in behalf of projects such as the youth development program of his native Tupelo, Mississippi, have been equally significant though infrequently publicized.

Elvis is noted for his strength of character. His loyalty to his friends is legendary. His long-standing contract with his manager consists of a mere handshake.

Elvis is married. He and his wife, Priscilla Ann have one daughter, Lisa Marie, age two and a half. They reside in Memphis, maintain a home in California.

1955, it was an unheard of amount. RCA didn't mind. The company executives who inked the deal knew a good investment when they saw one.

Whether Colonel Parker began his association with Elvis with the best of motives or not, Elvis' family basically feels that the two of them made a good pair. "I admired Colonel Tom for doing the things he did for Elvis," Donna says. "I don't think Elvis would have wanted to have any other life."

Elvis' friends from the projects had a different take on Colonel Parker, however. Elvis had remembered them and their friendship and had included the musicians from Lauderdale Courts on the bill at several of his shows. During those early years, Lee Denson saw the same old Elvis he always had been, "...a sweet, loving, adoring boy."

After Colonel Parker began working with Elvis, however, his friends thought Elvis had begun "to believe his press releases." Colonel Parker booked Elvis on *The Ed Sullivan Show* and the singer invited his friends from Lauderdale Courts, Jimmy and Lee Denson, to come along. After the show, they went up to Elvis' room. Colonel Parker answered the door, they said, and told them that no one could see Elvis. They told him they were Elvis' best friends. Colonel Parker's answer was for them to get out of the hall and out of the hotel. What really hurt, they recalled later, was that, if Elvis heard what was going on at the door, he didn't do anything to stop Colonel Parker from treating them that way.

But even as Elvis became more famous, made more money and had more people around him, he still wanted that security of having his family within easy reach. These were the people who had been with him from the start. These were the ones he could trust to be with him if it all fell apart. He couldn't be sure of anyone else, but he knew he could rely on his family. It's a good Southern tradition and the significance of it wasn't wasted on Elvis.

When he traveled to and lived in various places, some of his family members always went with him. One writer compared Elvis' moving his family around to the family in *The Grapes of Wrath*, always on the move and always together.

In fact, it might have been more like playing the board game "Risk." If you're smart, you don't invade new territory without first making a troop movement. You gather your forces and take them with you as you face new challenges. Then you always have them to fall back on if you are less than a success.

Thus, Elvis and several other Presleys, including his mother, father and grandmother, changed addresses a number of times in Memphis, finally ending up on a 14-acre estate with a nice enough house and room to bring more Presley troops if necessary.

The place was Elvis' new home, but he kept the name the former owner had given it. As of March, 1957, the official Presley address was Graceland.

3

"He truly was her life."

GRACELAND WAS MANY THINGS to Elvis. First, it was the fulfillment of that promise to buy a big house for his mother and father. The pink Cadillac, bought for Gladys' pleasure, that was parked outside meant that he had done what he had dreamed of doing.

Secondly, it was his home. It was a refuge from the crowds, the travel, the hustle that went with the new lifestyle he was living. Elvis loved being on stage, performing for his fans. But he loved being at this new home just as much. It was here that he could retreat, he could live with just his family again. When he needed the security and comfort that come with familiarity, he could go to Graceland and be there with his mother and father. Life could once again take on the feel that it had had in Tupelo and earlier in Memphis. At those times, it was Elvis, Vernon, Gladys and his grandmother Minnie alone against the world.

Within the walls of this house, when he was there with his family, Elvis had everything he needed in life. He could be at peace. He loved the house and he loved the setting. In fact, he was so enamored of the snow that they would get in Memphis that — should he be absent during a snowfall — Gladys and Vernon would make snowballs and freeze them for him to have when he returned.

One would imagine that Gladys would have been happy here. It was a lovely new home, certainly nicer than any she had had before. Outside was a brand new Cadillac, waiting to take her through the streets of Memphis, a way to go anywhere she wanted to be.

In truth, however, if she could have had the Cadillac take her anywhere she wanted to be, she would have put her family inside and taken them back to a time before Elvis Presley was a name that was on everyone's lips. It would be hard for most people to understand Gladys' reaction to Elvis' new-found fame. It's natural to assume that she would be proud of her son, thrilled with his success. The money he was making could buy his family things they never even dared to dream they would have. His celebrity status would open any door for them.

But in Gladys' mind, the celebrity closed a very important door — the one that linked her, her husband and her son in their own universe. The one that kept them together, just the three of them.

If Graceland was a realization of a fantasy for Gladys, it was no less the coming true of her worst nightmare. At a time when America probably envisioned her as one of the nation's happiest women, Gladys Presley was, in fact, one of its most conflicted.

Elvis seemed to enjoy his new status and still seemed genuinely to love his family. But Gladys found herself having to share her son with his fans, the press, with cameras, with adoring women. It was not a role she took to easily.

"Elvis' success sort of happened overnight," Donna says. "Gladys probably didn't have a chance to see it coming, to stop it or to get ready for it. I think that at some point she probably wished she had stopped it. When he got into show business and started having fans tearing his clothes off of him and trying to touch him, Aunt Gladys would be so upset. She'd say, 'They're going to kill my baby.' He always was her baby."

One of Elvis' friends from his days in Lauderdale Courts

in Memphis said that Elvis' fame literally made Gladys ill. The fans, who wanted to be a part of Elvis' life 24 hours a day, took her baby away from her. They and Colonel Parker stole the thing that was most important on earth to her.

To this point in Elvis' life, Gladys had been able to control his environment. If, as did happen once, Nash put him in a wagon and then let that wagon roll madly downhill, Gladys could give her a tongue-lashing that would stop such recklessness from going on ever again. Now Elvis seemed almost to be in another runaway wagon and this time, she couldn't do anything about it. If a reporter wrote something bad about him or if a fan stepped precariously close, well, a few well-placed words from his mother weren't going to change that at all.

Edie says that, even though she was a young child when Gladys died, she saw in her a woman "who found it very hard to let go of her son because he truly was her life."

Gladys, Edie says, "worried about everything. That kind of worrying you have to know how to cope with, and she didn't have the skills."

Gladys, family members say, turned to the only coping mechanism she knew — alcohol. If she was inclined to drink before — and all the family stories seem to bear that out — she now was driven to drink heavily. She sought a stupor that would let her shut out the changes in her world and, yet, she managed to hide her problem from most people. She seemed even to be able to hide it from her son. Whether he truly didn't know or just chose not to let himself know is a question that may never be answered.

Whatever method she used, Gladys did manage to dictate a relatively normal lifestyle for her family. Everything that happened at Graceland revolved around Elvis' schedule, but that didn't matter to Gladys and Vernon. They found as much happiness eating breakfast at 3 p.m. and spending the evening watching their son perform as other families found running on a more traditional schedule.

Just when Gladys had begun to settle into her new role as the mother of a star, something else happened to send her reeling, and this time she knew that she was powerless to change the course her son's life was about to take.

It was right before Christmas, 1957, at Graceland. Even in the swirl of activity around Elvis, there was a calm air at his home. Christmas always was special. There was a flurry of decorating and gift-buying, cooking and getting ready — then the peace of the season settled over the house and Gladys could almost forget about everything else that was going on.

That peace and feeling of security was shattered for her, though, when a man named Milton Bowers knocked on Graceland's door. He handed to Elvis a notice from the Memphis Draft Board #68. Elvis Aaron Presley was to report for induction into the United States Army at 7:45 a.m. on January 20, 1958.

It was a time that every mother in America knew probably would come to her son and, if she were truthful, an event each would tell you she dreaded. For Gladys, it was an event that turned her world upside down. For all the relatives' efforts to calm her down and to remind her that there wasn't a war going on, there was no consoling Gladys. She couldn't shake the fear that something bad would happen to Elvis while he was in the Army.

Vernon wasn't so happy about the whole thing either, Donna says. "But Elvis went on and did his duty. And he gained a lot of respect from people because of it. He did his job. He carried his weight. He was willing. Elvis grew up knowing that you do what is expected of you."

As it happened, Gladys and Vernon weren't the only ones who were afraid that something bad could happen to Elvis while he was away doing his patriotic duty. Colonel Tom Parker had an awful feeling that something could happen, too. Elvis was at the top of the entertainment world. He was in demand everywhere. Stores couldn't keep his records in stock, performances were "standing room only" and his movies created block-long lines at the box office.

Elvis always had feared that fame might be fleeting. Colonel Parker knew it was. Fame, he realized, could be the most fickle of lovers. While Elvis did his two-year stint in the Army, he wouldn't be making pictures, he wouldn't be cutting records and he wouldn't be appearing in front of mobs of screaming fans. Colonel Parker had seen it happen before — out of the fans' sight can be out of the fans' minds. And if another good–looking singer comes along in the meantime, the fans aren't always choosy about whose stage they throw their hotel room keys on.

He and Elvis talked about many approaches to take during this time in the Army. Elvis could have requested to do his time in a unit of entertainers who spent their service hours performing for those whose talent or name didn't earn them a place in Special Services. If he did this, he could live like a civilian and appear when the Army needed him. However, there was something in Elvis' upbringing that wouldn't let him do that.

Children of the South are brought up on God, country and apple pie. When it's your turn to do military duty, you do it, just like your father and his father and his father before him. You don't ask for special treatment and you don't look for a way out. You just do it. It's what you do because it's what you are supposed to do. That Deep South raising never left Elvis. And it never let him even think about doing his time in the Army any way but the Army way. If Uncle Sam wanted Elvis Presley, then Uncle Sam got Elvis Presley, 100 percent from the combat boots to the GI haircut. It would be one of the few times in Elvis' life when his clothes and hair looked just like everybody else's.

Given Elvis' determination to go soldiering, Colonel Parker began to think of ways to keep the home fires burning. He began stockpiling recordings so he could release Elvis Presley albums while the GI was doing his duty overseas. And he devised a public relations campaign that would keep Elvis' name in the newspapers and entertainment magazines. America would see the singing star on KP duty, getting inoculations, leaving for Germany, arriving in Germany, running obstacle courses and having meals in the mess hall. Wherever Elvis was on duty, there would be reporters and photographers on duty as well. Colonel Parker jokingly told a press conference that Elvis' change in career would mean a change in his income and a loss of hundreds of thousands of dollars in taxes for Uncle Sam. The Colonel, therefore, would make it his duty to see that Elvis stayed in a high tax bracket even while he was in the Army.

Elvis was filming *King Creole* when his draft notice arrived. In late December, 1957, he requested a deferment so he could finish the movie. Right after Christmas, he received notice that a 60-day deferment had been granted because of the expense that would be involved in remaking the almost-completed movie. His new date to report was March 20, 1958.

He marked the passing of 1957 and went back to California to finish *King Creole*. The movie wrapped and Elvis came back to Graceland to get ready for his induction.

It was early in the morning on March 24, 1958 and the Memphis Draft Board must have wondered if they had sent out notices to Elvis' entire family by mistake. Elvis arrived, accompanied by his parents, his Uncle Vester and his family, Colonel Parker, Elvis' girlfriend Anita Wood and a couple of other friends. Less than an hour later, Elvis Presley, singer and movie star, was Private Elvis Presley, serial number 53310761. By that afternoon, he was on a bus to Fort Chaffee, Arkansas, and a whole new phase of his life.

Elvis the civilian often kept upside–down hours, sleeping during the day, and working at night. Elvis the private heard Reveille at 5:30 a.m. March 25, 1958. It was the beginning of his first full day in the Army. Before it was over, a man named James B. Peterson would have cut one of the nation's most famous heads of hair and collected his fee for the thoroughly photographed event — 65 cents. The next day, Elvis got his uniform and his assignment. He would be stationed in Fort Hood, Texas, with the 2nd Armored Division.

When he arrived at Fort Hood, Elvis was assigned to Company A, 2nd Medium Tank Battalion, 37th Armor, 2nd Armored Division for basic training and advanced tank instruction. At the end of basic training, the new soldier was given a two-week leave and he went home to Graceland, home to the Memphis premiere of *King Creole*.

At the end of his leave, Elvis prepared to go back to Fort Hood. He carried his gear out the front door of Graceland, turned and closed the door behind him. He didn't know it then, but he had just left the Graceland he had known for the last time. The next time he stood in front of those doors, everything would have changed.

A young Gladys and Vernon Presley.

Elvis beams at two of his favorite "girls,"
grandmother Dodger and daughter Lisa Marie.

Elvis with his cousins Susie, left, and
Donna in the back yard of Graceland.

Vernon drives his El Camino at the Circle G Ranch in Walls, Mississippi, about 30 miles from Graceland.

The view of the back of Graceland from Vernon's office. This entrance is the one the family used.

Graceland's front drive and lawn.

The stairway that led to Elvis' bedroom at Graceland.

A gift from Lisa Marie to her daddy.

Dodger and newborn
Lisa Marie.

Priscilla and Lisa Marie.   Lisa Marie and her stuffed friends.

Lisa Marie all dolled up in fur.

Dodger's Bible and pearls on her bedside table at Graceland.

Dodger, Vernon and their landlady near the home they shared with Elvis when he was stationed in Germany.

Dodger wearing one of her signature aprons. Grandson Elvis made sure she had an apron to match every dress.

Dodger inside Elvis' home in Bad Homburg, Germany.

Dodger and her sister, Alice.

Vester and his car which nephew Elvis gave him.

A young Delta.

Delta, Edmond I (dog shared by Delta and Elvis) and Rising Sun (Elvis' horse). (Photo by David McGough.)

Susie and Donna while visiting Graceland.

Susie, Earl and Donna in front of Graceland.

Two-year-old Jamie and granddaddy Earl and mother Donna in front of Graceland, 1978.

Donna in 1968, the year she graduated from high school.

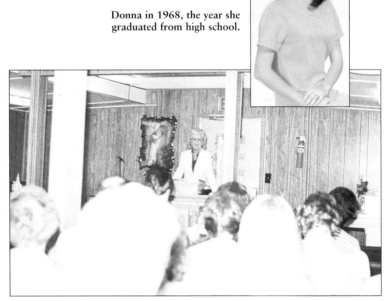

Nash at her church in Walls, Mississippi.

Jamie and Stacy in front of grandmother Nash's car at Graceland.

Earl at Graceland.

Alice Hood Hacker, an Elvis cousin who was Edie's
grandmother and Dodger's niece.

Edie's grandparents Walter and Alice Hacker
(Elvis' cousin) on their 50th wedding
anniversary.

Earl mows the front lawn at Graceland.

Elvis' paternal grandfather, Jesse, with his second wife, Vera.

Vernon lounges in the sun at Graceland, with Earl in the background.

One of Elvis' first guitars.

"I would give up everything...
if it would bring my mama back."

WHEN ELVIS RETURNED TO Fort Hood, he quickly became just one of the guys. He often said that, when he first entered the Army, he had thought the other men in his unit might give him a hard time. But they didn't once they saw that he was going to do the same things they did, work just as hard as anyone else and not ask for any special favors.

In mid-June, 1958, however, he did ask for one thing. The Army had a provision allowing dependents of a soldier to live in the city where he was stationed. Elvis definitely was the breadwinner of the Presley family by this time and he requested that his family be allowed to move to Texas.

The Army probably was just as glad that Elvis had made the request. While Elvis was on the inside at Fort Hood, behaving like any other GI, his fans were on the outside. Whether it was that Colonel Parker was doing a good job keeping Elvis' name in the public eye or whether Elvis would have stayed "hot" regardless is a matter for discussion. Whatever the reason, the Army suddenly found itself surrounded by young girls — many of them wearing lipstick in such colors as Tender Pink and Houndog Orange — all willing to risk just about anything short of treason for the chance to get on the base where Elvis was training as an armor crew-man.

If Elvis lived off base with his family, he would be some-one else's security responsibility for at least part of the day, the Army must have reasoned. Elvis' request was approved. Gladys and Vernon joined their son in Texas, living in a rented three-bedroom trailer. Security immediately became a prob-lem. The trailer now became the focal point for all the fans' aspirations of meeting Elvis. It wasn't long before Elvis had sought out a home in Killeen and moved his parents and his grandmother Minnie there. Here, at least, his family could have a little bit of privacy. It wasn't like Graceland, but they all were together. It wasn't an arrangement that would last.

In August, Gladys' health began to fail and she saw sev-eral doctors in Texas. When she continued to get worse, Vernon decided she should go home to Memphis and see her own doctors there. Elvis drove his family to the train station and watched as the railroad car carrying his family pulled away.

When Gladys arrived in Memphis the next day, she im-mediately was admitted to Methodist Hospital. It's pretty much agreed among the family that she had hepatitis, prob-ably brought on by the alcohol she had consumed in her anxiety over the path her son's life had taken.

Three days later, Elvis was granted emergency leave to be with his mother, whose health by this time had declined to the point that she was terminally ill.

Memphis in August is hot and sticky. It's the kind of hot that slaps you in the face, soaks your freshly donned shirt within minutes after you step out the door and squeezes you so tightly that you can hardly breathe.

It was that kind of heat that was waiting for Elvis as he got off the plane from Texas on August 12, 1958, and headed to the car his father had waiting. But it wasn't the heat that was taking his breath away, it was the prospect of what he would find when he got to his mother's hospital room.

So many times he had come back to Memphis from tours or from Hollywood and he always headed to Graceland and the comfort that his own home offered. Now Vernon turned the car not in the direction of home, but towards the hospital. He knew that having Elvis there would help Gladys and he knew that with Gladys was the only place Elvis wanted to be.

During that first visit, Elvis could only bring himself to stay in Gladys' room for a few minutes. He was an actor, but he wasn't that good. He couldn't hide from his mother the sense of impending doom that must have washed over him when he saw her lying there. He walked out the door and sat down in a chair in the hall. Elvis put his head in his hands and wept openly. He was crying for his mother, his father, himself and for the helplessness he felt. Surrounded by people, he was utterly and completely alone.

One of the things that members of Elvis' family had learned quickly after he became a star was that privacy was a thing of the past. Elvis found it impossible to visit his mother without creating a commotion in the hospital, on the street outside and in front of Graceland, so he tried to keep his visits brief and spaced far enough apart so that the hospital could recover from one before he arrived for another.

He came to see his mother several times during the day of August 13. His last visit ended about midnight and he went to Graceland to try to sleep. Sleep probably didn't come easily to him, though. He had become accustomed to the routine of life in Fort Hood. Now that routine was broken which, in itself, was enough to deny him his rest. Added to that was the worry about his mother.

He probably was awake when the phone rang shortly after 3 a.m. It was Vernon. He thought Elvis should come to the hospital right away.

Vernon was waiting in the hall outside Gladys' room when Elvis rushed onto the floor. He looked at his son and told him, "She's gone." Elvis' eyes only met Vernon's for a moment and then he hurried into his mother's room. Gladys indeed was gone. Silently, in the middle of the night, the anchor that held Elvis' life in place had slipped away. For the first time ever, he was adrift. He had no direction, no goal, no inspiration. He had lost the person he had lived for.

He lay across his mother's body and cried for a very long time. Finally convinced to let her go, he joined his father for the ride back to Graceland. It was not the same Elvis Presley who returned to Graceland that day. The public may not have noticed, because Elvis — as well as the rest of the family — was very talented when it came to presenting a "public face." As he once told Edie, "We are a family with all these different masks and those of us that are the best become masters of disguises."

But the people who really understood Elvis knew how much he had changed. Donna was eight years old, living in Missouri with her parents on that day that would change Elvis so much, and remembers that, "when Aunt Gladys died, Mom and Dad went to Memphis to be with Elvis, Uncle Vernon and Grandma.

"Susie (Karen Sue, Donna's sister) and I were children, so we stayed with my Dad's parents until they came back home. I know from the things Mom told me after she got back that Elvis was heartbroken when his mother died."

Nash knew from the first moment she and her husband, Earl, drove up Graceland's driveway that Elvis was going to need a lot of comfort during the days that followed his mother's death. When they arrived, Elvis was outside, walking up and down in front of Graceland, holding one of his mother's gowns. Nash sat with Elvis on the porch at Graceland and had a long talk about Gladys' dying. Elvis was looking for answers, for support. Nash didn't have all the answers, but she did give him the love and support she had cultivated when they were young together. Nash told Donna that Elvis cried often during the days after Gladys' death. Nash remembered:

He said, "Aunt Nash, why? I've got millions of dollars, but I would give up everything and gladly go back to digging ditches if it would bring my mama back."

Because he was an only child, Elvis felt his mother and father were all that he had. "Now, he had lots of family that loved him, but this was just about his immediate family. He had a mother and a daddy. He had no brothers or sisters," Donna says. "So his parents were his whole life as well. Everything he did, everything he bought was for them." His sense of loss was deepened, because he had lost half of everything he felt really was his.

"His life changed after that. There was always a sadness in Elvis after that," Donna says. "You could see that sadness in him."

So great was his loss that Elvis reasoned he never could endure such a thing again. "He was an extremely passionate person and the love he had for his mother and father was so great that he said he wanted to die first because he didn't think he could stand to lose one of them," Donna remembers. "After his mother died, he said he hoped he died before his father because he couldn't handle losing another loved one."

On the afternoon of August 14, 1958, Gladys Love Smith Presley came home to Graceland one last time. Her body lay in state there that evening. The next day, Elvis and his father led a solemn procession to the funeral home where 400 invited guests paid their final respects to the woman from Tupelo, Mississippi, who had become the mother of a legend.

After the funeral, Gladys was buried in Forest Hill Cemetery, about three miles from Graceland. Elvis visited her grave often, taking the chance to be close to her, to talk to her again. Wilbert McGhee, a Forest Hill employee, often watched as Elvis rode up on a motorcycle and headed for his mother's grave. Elvis seemed mindful that McGhee was one of the people who watched over Gladys' grave when her son wasn't there. He took the time to smile and wave when he saw McGhee. That was one thing about Elvis. No matter how sad he was feeling at the time, he managed to have a smile for the people he felt were helping him.

Gladys' death was a pivotal point in Elvis' life. He never got over the feelings that he had that day at Graceland. More than a decade later, he talked to Edie about grief. Edie's 19-year-old brother, David, had been killed in an automobile accident and she was going through all of the emotions people experience after losing a loved one. Edie, who was 22 at the time, felt guilty because she hadn't been with David the way she was supposed to have been.

Edie felt she had been responsible for David. He was living with her in Florence, Alabama, at the time. She was in college and he was working. David had left Florence that night to go see his girlfriend perform in a play in a small North Alabama town not far from Florence. Edie was supposed to go, but changed her mind at the last minute. David went alone and was driving by himself, overtired and determined to get home. Edie thought that if she had been with him, he wouldn't have been driving when he was so tired. She was convinced that she was the reason for her brother's death.

She had had a brother who helped her think through decisions, who could bring a smile to her face when she felt down. Now she had one thing left — a ring he had bought her. A few months earlier, Edie had gone with David to pick out an engagement ring for his girlfriend. Edie didn't know it at the time, but he also had picked out a ring for her. He bought it as a surprise gift for his sister. Now it seemed to be her one unbroken link to him.

She felt anger, she felt sadness and she sank into a depression that left her unable to go on with her life. Her grandmother Alice Hacker knew that Elvis would understand her feelings, so she conspired to get the two of them together.

Grandma Hacker sent Edie to Memphis to attend a Blackwood Brothers concert with Susie, who was living at Graceland with Nash and Earl at the time. Before the concert, Edie went over to visit with Minnie for a while. They talked a few minutes and then Minnie said, "You know Elvis is upstairs and he really was saddened to hear about David."

"Grandma said it might help me to talk to him," Edie remembers telling Minnie. "Then she said, 'You know, it might be good for both of you.' She called him on the phone and he said for me to come on upstairs."

When Edie walked into Elvis' room, "he just got up and came to me and hugged me. I saw that he was emotional. He had tears in his eyes. He asked me why I was in Memphis. I told him that Susie and I were going to a concert. After that, we talked about light things, dating and such.

"I didn't realize I was doing it, but I kept rubbing that ring that David had bought for me. Elvis must have noticed, though. He put his hand over my hand and said, 'And why else are you here?'

"I told him I was hoping to see him because my grandmother had said he could understand the pain I was having over David's death. By this time, tears were rolling down his cheeks and I was crying, too."

Elvis looked at Edie and said, "All the fame, all the money, these material things are nothing when it comes to crossing that road between life and death. The most valuable thing you could ever have in this world is love and I had everything rolled up in Mama.

"She told me from the time I was a little boy that I was special and I was going to be somebody special and when the kids laughed at me, I should never be anything but who I am. I compared Mama to a rose. There will be other roses in your life. Even though things seem awful dark right now there will be a time when you find another rose, but you'll never forget that one."

His mother's impact on his life, he said, had been love. He said she taught him the deepest of all love and the respect for mankind.

"He said he cut himself off after his mother died," Edie says. "He said he understood how I wanted to cut myself off and not love again so I wouldn't be hurt again, but he said that he had learned that love was out there."

Edie told Elvis that one of the things she missed most about David was that "he was the one I shared all my dreams and all my hopes with."

"That's the way it was with my mama. I shared all my dreams and all my hopes. And to imagine that I could achieve all this is beyond my wildest dreams," Elvis told her.

"It was hours of both of us crying, sharing pain," Edie says. That day, Elvis told her that he believed "that there are some people in this world who we really connect with in life and that even death is just another window. They may not be here physically with us, but they're with us.

"Edie, they are just a window away," Elvis said. "David is always going to be with you. Mama's with me, right here. He's with you."

"That day, I saw a real compassion in Elvis. He said he had come to a place where he could always be with the spirit of his mother, where he could talk to her and cry with her and he did that every day," Edie says. "He got through to me. I talked to my grandmother not long after that. She was milking and we were talking about life. I told her about what Elvis had said. She just said, 'I'm so glad.'

"He took my pain that day and turned it around into something to give me hope," Edie remembers. "After I talked to Elvis, I went back to college. That was the best year of my school life. Each time I was in a play, Elvis would send me two dozen yellow roses with a note that said, 'I am there with you and so is David.' "

The advice Elvis gave Edie that day didn't come to him on the spur of the moment. He often thought about death in general and Gladys' death in particular. He sought a constructive way to deal with his mother's death. But, at times, he was overwhelmed by the loss.

Once, a number of years after Gladys' death, Nash left her home on the Graceland property to walk over to the main house and talk to Minnie. Nash recalled that day:

I had gotten a few feet out in the yard, I looked up and saw Elvis standing there by the fence that surrounds the pasture. I stood there a minute and watched him because I wasn't sure if he wanted to be alone. He seemed to be in deep thought. He finally turned around and motioned for me to come on out there. (I guess he sensed my presence.) I went on over and put my arm around his waist. He put one arm over my shoulders and we both looked out at the pasture.

I said, "Is everything okay?" But he didn't say anything, so I said, "A penny for your thoughts." He laughed and said, "I'm not sure they are worth a penny."...Then he asked me what I saw when I looked out at the pasture.

I said, "I see the pasture, the horses, the big barn and the small barn." He said, "What else?" I said, "I see the racquetball court, the office, the tractors, the old black truck." He said, "What else?" By this time, I was running out of anything to see, but I said, "I see Vernon's house, the back of the fence and I can see part of the swimming pool, why?"

He told me I was missing the point. By then, I figured he probably was seeing something in his mind that wasn't actually there. I said, "Why don't you tell me what you see?" He said, "I see Mama and Daddy riding in the golf cart and Lisa is between them." Then he said, "Oh, dear God, why couldn't it have been?"

He told me that Gladys was looking forward to her first grandchild. He said he would like for Gladys to know how cute and special Lisa was.

5

"They didn't want him to
be by himself."

SOMEHOW, AS EDIE POINTS out, Elvis managed to pull himself together — at least outwardly — after his mother's death. The Army was willing to give him emergency leave when Gladys was sick and for a while after she died, but regardless of how much that event had affected him, Elvis the soldier was going to have to report back to his post before long.

So, ten days after his mother died, Elvis was back at Fort Hood. Two weeks later, the Associated Press wires clattered in newsrooms around the nation. It wasn't "stop the presses" kind of news, but it was news nonetheless. Elvis Presley, the AP dutifully reported, had been assigned to the 3rd Armored Division in Germany as a truck driver. Things were moving quickly in Elvis' life now. On September 19, 1958, a week after the announcement was made, the young GI was standing by the train ready to leave for the Military Ocean Terminal in Brooklyn, New York. That would be his "jumping off place" on the way to Germany. There to see Elvis off were Vernon, Minnie, Anita Wood and several of Elvis' friends. Of course, there also were as many fans as could find a way to be in the vicinity of the train as it pulled away from the station in Texas.

Three days later, Elvis' train arrived in New York. Once

91

again, there were walls of fans, many of whom had signed a petition to get the Army to change its mind about sending Elvis anywhere. When that didn't work, they apparently decided that if Elvis was leaving, he was going to have one of the biggest send-offs the Army had ever seen. Amid a great deal of hoop-la (official and unofficial), Elvis and more than 1100 other GIs finally left for Germany aboard the *USS General Randall.*

On October 1, the ship docked at Bremerhaven, West Germany. Perhaps the Army thought they had left Elvis-mania behind and maybe even waved it a fond farewell as the *Randall* left New York. If they did, they were in for a major disappointment when the ship arrived in Germany. Elvis' European fans were determined to give him as big a welcome there as the goodbye had been from his American fans in New York. There were the same sights and sounds that the Army had begun to expect whenever Elvis was around — girls screaming and swooning for as far as the eye could see, television cameras rolling, flashbulbs popping. The only difference anyone could discern was that the girls were screaming, "We love you" in a different language.

Edie, a second grader at the time, watched Elvis' arrival in Germany on the six o'clock news on Channel 9 from her home in Red Bay, Alabama. For all the television and newspaper coverage, the event seemed to glide by an eight-year-old Donna and five-year-old Susie. Mostly, they remember their mother and father discussing how Vernon and Minnie were going to Germany to be with Elvis while he was over there "because it was so close to his mother's death and they didn't want him to be by himself."

When the other Presleys, accompanied by some of Elvis' friends, arrived in Germany the day after Elvis did, they didn't get nearly as much fanfare and publicity, which was fine with them. They settled in to begin their life in Germany. Over at the base, Elvis was getting his assignment — to Company D, 1st Battalion, 32nd Armor, 3rd Armored Division of the 7th Army as a jeep driver for Lt. Col. Henry Grimm.

Of course, even in Germany, Elvis' hair was a hot topic.

His basic training cut had grown out, but he still had to maintain a military look. He sought out someone to become his regular barber. He found Karl-Heinz Stein, the head "hair-cutter" at the base where Elvis was stationed. One day a soft-spoken new soldier arrived at Stein's shop. Stein recognized his new customer — it would have been hard not to — and was a little nervous about the haircut. Putting Elvis into 100 percent military trim took about 10 or 15 minutes. The barber handed Elvis a mirror and asked if the haircut was okay. Elvis nodded his approval and asked how much his tab was. He owed 35 cents for the cut, but handed the barber a dollar and told him to keep the change.

Elvis came back about twice every month for the next 17 months. He sat and read comic books during his haircuts. Sometimes Elvis would laugh out loud if he got to a particularly good part.

For years after Elvis left Germany, Stein kept the chair Elvis had sat in and the scissors and straight razor he had used on the famous locks. Other soldiers who came to Germany after Elvis got to enjoy some of the notoriety as well. They'd tell their wives and girlfriends, "Hey, Elvis' barber cuts my hair."

Before much of October was gone, Elvis and his family had moved two times. They first lived in a three-bedroom apartment in Hotel Bruenwald in Bad Homburg and then settled into a four-bedroom house at 14 Goethestrasse. A sign quickly went up outside, designating the times of day when Elvis would sign autographs. It wasn't typical Army issue, but then Elvis wasn't typical Army, no matter how much he might have tried to be.

A routine soon established itself at the Presley house. Elvis spent his days on base and his nights at home, usually having a party or entertaining fans. His taste for Southern cooking hadn't changed and he ate every meal he could at home. The rest he took on base. In fact, the only taste Elvis had of foreign food during his whole stay overseas was the food he had while he was on leave in Paris. Elvis figured that if turnip greens, cornbread and fried chicken had gotten his family through to this point, there really was no need in his life for sauerbraten, klopse and Lebkuchen. Elvis already knew the kinds of foods he liked and how he liked them prepared. His taste buds, just like the rest of him, were rooted in the Deep South and not about to make any foreign journeys.

If the cuisine didn't necessarily appeal to Elvis, something else the country had to offer did. The young ladies of Germany were just as beautiful and just as in awe of Elvis as the ones he had left behind in the United States. Many of them found their way to the Presley home and partied with Elvis and his friends there. Vernon and Minnie got used to having the girls, the friends and the parties around. Even they were a little taken aback, however, when a new girl showed up a few months before Elvis was scheduled to go back to the States.

She was different from the rest — definitely younger, obviously much more shy and noticeably quieter than most of the other girls they had met. Priscilla Beaulieu, an Army brat and barely a teenager, presented new challenges for Elvis. He had to go meet her father, an Army captain. He had to agree to certain arrangements for picking Priscilla up and bringing her home. Why would a man who could have had any girl on the continent with just the snap of his fingers agree to all of Priscilla's father's conditions? He saw something special in Miss Beaulieu. He might not have known it right away, but it was going to be a something that he couldn't get out of his mind.

Germany brought Elvis in touch with Priscilla, a person who would bring light to him and his entire family. Nash and some of the rest of Elvis' family fear that it also might have been during his stay in Germany that something dark came into Elvis' life. There, they think, Elvis took the first steps into a vicious cycle that would haunt him the rest of his life. His parties often lasted well into the mornings. When he had to report for duty, he would need something to help him wake up. Somehow, he found the pills that would do that. Often, when he needed to unwind, he was too keyed up from the day to sleep. He found something to help him with that, too. Nash said in a television interview she did several years after Elvis' death that she felt this was when his health started to fail and probably when he started using — and eventually misusing — prescription drugs.

On January 20, 1959, Elvis Presley was promoted to sergeant. He proudly displayed his new stripes for the press photographers and the television cameramen. He had done what he set out to do when he joined the Army. He had put in his time in the service, obeyed the rules and had been a heads-up soldier. As his reward, the Army put him in command of a three-man reconnaissance team.

He had done his patriotic duty. He had met a special young woman. In many ways, Elvis' stay in Germany had been a success. Elvis had learned one thing in his short life, however. It seemed that there always were conflicts. Just when he should be at his happiest, something would come along to make him wonder if the good things that were happening to him were worth it all. After he became a singing star, he lost his mother. When he met Priscilla, his father met someone new as well. Dee Stanley, the soon-to-be ex-wife of a military man, and her three sons came into Elvis' life.

If ever Elvis' feelings were in turmoil, it was now. He wanted more than anything for his father to be happy and Dee seemed to make him happy. On the other hand, there was the matter of Gladys. Elvis couldn't really imagine anyone taking his mother's place in his father's life. As far as Elvis was concerned, there was and would be only one Mrs. Vernon Presley and his mother was it. It was difficult to see his father with Dee when he so wished he could be seeing him with Gladys. Still, it was obvious to everyone that Vernon was in love with Dee. When they announced that they were getting married, it was official. Elvis would have a stepmother and, for the first time in his life, stepbrothers. It may have taken him a while, but he did adjust to the idea and began to take Dee and her sons under his wing. They were part of his family. He considered taking care of them one of his responsibilities.

In early February, 1960, Minnie returned to Memphis.

Elvis would be discharged soon and he would be back home at Graceland. She went to get the house ready for his return. On March 2, Vernon and the rest of the Presley entourage started their journey home. That same day, Elvis left Frankfurt for the United States and by the next morning, he was in New Jersey. It was snowing when Elvis got off the plane, but he didn't mind. Elvis always enjoyed the snow at Graceland and these flurries reminded him that he soon would be walking through those familiar, comfortable doors. His fans didn't mind either. They were there, in the snow, waiting to greet him. Elvis had to realize that his fears of being forgotten were unfounded. His fans had waited patiently, expectantly, for him and finally, they were being rewarded. Elvis was back on home soil!

Elvis headed for the railroad station and the train that would take him back to Memphis. He had leased a private railroad car for him and the friends and members of his family who were traveling with him. It would be best to travel that way, he had reasoned. Otherwise, there would be havoc throughout the train with people trying to see him and talk to him. He could have a little privacy this way and probably save the railroad some money on the repairs that would have to be done after the crowd got through with its train cars.

His privacy, though, was about to be invaded by two old friends. William Leaptrott, his friend from the Lauderdale Courts days, and Bill Burk, another friend from Elvis' teenage years, were working for *The Memphis Press-Scimitar* and they had a plan for getting on the train and in for an interview with their old pal. They drove to the last stop the train made before Memphis, bought tickets and began searching out Elvis' car.

When they got there, some of Elvis' traveling companions were ready to turn them away. Elvis ushered them in, though, and they got their time to talk with him.

Elvis truly was excited about coming back home to Memphis. He was so excited, in fact, that his fellow travelers noticed a change in him as the train neared the station. The closer Elvis got to home, the more nervous he became. Surely there were many things on Elvis' mind. Would the fans really welcome him and his music with open arms? Could his popularity really have withstood all the challenges to it that arose while he was away? That alone was enough to make him nervous. Then there was the other thing. What was Graceland going to be like without Gladys? Could he ever really feel at home there again? Or would he just be haunted by the memories of the few months his mother had been able to live in the house he had bought for her?

Anyone returning from the service probably looks forward to a good, home-cooked meal and a chance to kick back and slip happily into civilian life. Elvis wanted those things, too. He just couldn't be sure how much he would be able to enjoy them without his mother sharing his good times.

Whatever lay ahead was about to begin. The train was almost ready to pull into the Memphis station. Elvis, who had worn his Army uniform on the journey back home, stepped into an adjoining room and changed into his civilian clothes. The Elvis the fans had known was back — and, once again, you could recognize him by what he wore. He smiled and stepped off the train. His fans were there to greet him. Even if they didn't allay all of his fears, they did make him feel welcome. He rushed to the waiting car and waved as the vehicle pulled away from the station and turned to go to Graceland.

It was March 7, 1960. Elvis was home — back at Graceland. None of the horrible things Gladys had feared might happen to Elvis had come to pass. The one thing neither of them dared to think about had happened. Gladys had been a part of everything Elvis did before he went to Germany. Now he was back in Memphis, 25 years old, essentially starting his life all over again. This second part of his life would be different. One of the people he counted on most was gone. It wasn't going to be easy. But he would have to try.

In Missouri, Donna and Susie had traced Elvis' journey back through the news clips. Of course, they followed the news not to learn about a superstar, but to find out when a family member would be getting home. As soon as Elvis was back at Graceland, Nash and her family would be going to Tennessee to visit him. It was a journey like those made by families all over the United States. The soldier boy was home and a proper welcome was in order. Nash gathered her two girls and they headed to Graceland. At the end of the bus trip, they caught a cab to the mansion. Ordinarily, they would have gone in the back door. That's what family did when they came to Graceland, but the taxi let them out at the front door. Nash and her charges walked up the steps and rang the bell.

"Elvis answered the door himself," Donna remembers. "He was dressed in a black shirt and black pants and I remember thinking that he was very handsome." The house, naturally, was full of people. Elvis was having a party to celebrate coming home. "We hugged and kissed Elvis and then went to Grandma's room."

If Nash and the rest of the family had managed to bring any semblance of normalcy to their lives while Elvis was away, it all went out the back door of Graceland when Elvis stepped in at the front.

6

"There always was excitement
for everyone who lived there."

PEOPLE WHO VISIT GRACELAND today see it in a sterile state. It's really a museum now. But once, it was a house, a home, a living, breathing being. As Nash put it, "There always was excitement for everyone who lived there."

When Elvis came home from Germany, Graceland became its own universe. Try to think of it that way, a cosmic entity with two suns. Minnie was the larger of the two, with a magnetic pull that could overcome even that of the other sun, Elvis. Around her, the family planets revolved. Things were done at Graceland Minnie's way. And Elvis was content with that arrangement. After all, he was gone so much and she was there all the time. It was only right that she be in charge. When Elvis was absent from Graceland, the family members and staff there moved in steady, even orbits around Minnie. When he did reappear, the pull of his personality sent things spinning a little out of control. Most of the family still tried to maintain their equilibrium, steadied by Minnie, but Elvis' charisma was so great that, inevitably, they found themselves moving in ovals, coming close to Minnie at times, close to Elvis at others. It wasn't bad. It was just a little like getting on the Tilt-A-Whirl at the fair. It was thrilling while you were riding, dizzying when you got off.

"Elvis longed for Graceland when he was away," Donna says. "It was where he could be himself. He could be the private Elvis at Graceland."

Unless you are a family member, it is a little difficult to understand how quickly everyone at Graceland could accept a new definition of "normal." Some days, your life ran on the same cycle as everyone else's. Other days, you got up at midnight and went to bed at noon. "We never had what other people would call a normal life," Donna says. "But to us, it was just the way things were. It was normal to us."

Living or visiting at Graceland could mean being a participant in or the victim of elaborate, expensive practical jokes. It could mean going to the amusement park or the mall or the movie in the middle of the night. Or you might find yourself going on a car shopping expedition late at night, coming home in one of a dozen or so cars that Elvis had purchased. You might be riding horses one week and racing golf carts the next. It was nothing if not exciting when Elvis was at home.

Bringing some sort of calm to the whole thing was Minnie, who presided from her room at Graceland. If ever anyone was qualified for the job, it was Minnie Mae Hood Presley. Tall and stern-looking, Minnie had married Jesse Presley when she was a young woman. It didn't take her long to realize that Jesse had some traits that no woman would want in her husband. He was prone to drink and he was prone to wander. There were other women in Jesse's life almost from the first of their marriage. Minnie accepted a great deal of what Jesse dealt out without saying much, however, and their marriage produced five children. Had Minnie known how much Jesse's womanizing would hurt their youngest child, Nash, she might have taken on the challenge of straightening him out rather than just looking the other way.

When Nash was in the second grade, her father was "seeing" the mother of two of her classmates. The two girls knew Jesse was married and that he was at their mother's house as much or more than he was home. And they knew Nash was his child. Worse than that, they knew that Minnie was struggling to feed and clothe her children while Jesse spent his money on them and their mother. They didn't let Nash forget it, either. They teased her constantly, showing her new things that Jesse had bought for them. Nash missed most of her second grade year at school because she couldn't bring herself to go and face those children.

Jesse's behavior made for an up and down sort of childhood for his children. As Nash explained:

> We had good times, bad times, happy times and sad times and we accepted it all as part of life.
> Our dad was a hard worker and he helped to build a strong character in his five children.
> He taught us to work hard for what we wanted in life. He taught us to stand straight and tall, to have a good smile, to dress neatly. And all the while, he was creating a lifestyle of drinking and womanizing for himself.

Eventually, Jesse's drinking and womanizing were just too much. He and Minnie went their separate ways. Even though their children were grown, it still hurt them. Nash said:

> I loved my dad very much, but it tore me apart to see what he was doing to my mom. I remember one time I was going somewhere with my daddy and I was sitting there in the truck watching him as he drove because he had been drinking.
> I was just a little girl, but I said, "Daddy, you need to get saved and quit drinking because we love you and we don't like to see you drink." He patted me on the leg and said, "Baby, if you keep praying for me, someday I'm sure I will."
> He did get saved, but only after he had left my mom...You always are so thankful when a member

*of your family gets saved...but it seems a shame there
has to be a breakup in the home before it happens...*

*When we went to Louisville, Kentucky, when my
dad passed away...my stepmother, Vera, and her son
and daughter-in-law spoke very highly of my dad. I
felt very hurt that they had gotten to share a part of
my daddy's life that I didn't get to share.*

With the absence of a father that would be what Minnie
perceived as a positive influence on the children, she under-
took to be sure her offspring grew up with good, solid values. They would learn a work ethic and they would know
the Bible. If she couldn't give them an ideal family life, Minnie
reasoned, she would give her children roots that would see
them through these hard times and others that might come.
Nash put it this way:

*Our mother was a wonderful woman. She was
the one who taught us to have a strong faith in God,
to look to Him for our daily strength and to lean on
Him...She taught us to read the Bible and to read it
every day...*

*She was a strong lady in more ways than one. She
was the peacemaker and said on many occasions, "If
you can't make peace, don't break it."*

*She believed that idle hands were the devil's work-
shop and she always kept busy. She would spend a
lot of time working out in the yard.*

*She put out a garden every year. It seemed she felt
closer to God when she worked in the soil. It helped
to put food on our table and she communed with
God as she worked...*

*Mom kept our house so clean you could have eaten
off the floors. She milked the cows, gave slop to the
hogs and churned the milk to make butter...I would
sit there, leaning up against a post of the porch, and
think how lucky I was to have a mother like her. Mom
always dressed neatly and smelled so clean and good...*

She would get up in the mornings, see that we were fed and then go out to the field and help Daddy. Then she would come in, cook a good dinner and go out on the porch to visit with the neighbors...

Vester said to her one time, "Why do you go out in the field and work? You know you don't have to." She said, "Son, I know I don't have to, I just want to."...I think she got many of her problems solved while pulling weeds and praying...

The Bible laying on Mom's bedside table introduced our family to what Jesus Christ was really like...The pair of Mom's pearls laying on top represented the pearls of wisdom that were ours when we prayed to God to give us an understanding heart and mind. The handkerchief tucked inside was Mom's and it reminded us of the relaxed way she accepted what God was teaching her...

She was about six feet tall and every bit of her being was devoted to God, to caring for her family and to reaching out to others.

She was love in motion, with a quiet, sweet, gentle and humble spirit. She was our close and trusted friend. She was a gracious lady and a virtuous woman. With a God-given wisdom, she guided us through hardships and heartaches and taught us to look to God for our strength.

Nash recalled the time Elvis talked to Minnie about Jesse:

I remember Elvis talking to my mom one time about my Dad. He said, "Dodger, I know it's been rough on you with your home being broken up after you've brought up five children and you've had your own home for so many years. But you are here with me and Daddy just lives across the pasture. Aunt Nash lives out back just a few feet from us and Aunt Delta is here with us. We are going to enjoy life, so don't be hurt anymore and if you have any bitterness, let God take it out and wrap you in His love."

Minnie's experiences with Jesse didn't so much make her bitter as they made her tough. She became a woman who would speak her mind no matter what the subject or who was listening. But that was one thing that endeared her to her family. They knew she was telling them the truth, because they'd never known her to sugarcoat anything. If she said you looked good in a certain dress, you looked good in it. If you were doing something foolish, she'd point that out to you.

She didn't spare the honesty when it came to Elvis. Once, Donna remembers, he thought it would be a good idea for Minnie to have a hot plate in her bedroom. "The maids fixed her meals and brought them to her and everything, but Elvis thought it would be nice if she had a hot plate in there to keep things warm if she wanted to," she recalls. "So he gave her a hot plate for Christmas. It made her mad. I guess Elvis learned right then that you don't give women practical gifts. She told him, 'I wanted some money for Christmas.' So he goes upstairs and brings down a few hundred dollars and says, 'Dodger, if you ever want money, all you have to do is ask me for it.' She took that money and threw it down on the floor. She told him she didn't want it if she had to ask for it. He was supposed to know that's what she wanted."

Once when Minnie and Donna were talking about Jesse, she told her granddaughter that "she had never kissed my grandfather or any other man on the lips. Can you imagine? Five kids, but never one kiss on the mouth," Donna laughs. "I was absolutely floored. When I asked her why, she said that was unclean."

Another time, Minnie told Donna that Jesse never had divorced her, that he had just left. Donna, who thinks most things can be made right by a simple application of the law or some logic, told her that they should report him. By now he had a new wife and, as Donna pointed out, "that's against the law." Minnie looked at her granddaughter and said, "Why would I want to do that? If she wants him, she's welcome to him." The discussion was over.

Another time, Jesse made an appearance on the television game show *I've Got A Secret*. Donna and Minnie happened to be watching the show that night. As the panelists unraveled Jesse's secret, they figured out that he was a member of Elvis' family and one female member of the panel gushed, "You can't be his grandfather! You're much too young!" Jesse beamed as Garry Moore said, "That's right, he's Elvis Presley's grandfather." Back at Graceland, Minnie nodded toward the screen and said, "Just look at that damned fool up there." There was to be no more talk about Jesse and his fifteen minutes of fame.

As a teenager, Donna spent a lot of time at Graceland — much of it with Minnie. She and her Grandma were pals. They enjoyed the hours they had together. A lot of those hours were spent in front of the television set. Minnie sort of held court from the red chair in her bedroom. When he was growing up, Elvis had promised to buy her a red armchair to put in the big house he was going to own. Now she had that chair and it was a little like the throne of Graceland. Minnie handed down her rulings and opinions — good, bad and otherwise — from her seat in that chair. She didn't spend all of her time there. "Grandma and I would laugh and joke and dance. We'd listen to music and she'd dance around the room with me. We'd have a ball," Donna remembers.

The chair was one of her favorite places, though, because it was the place from which she watched television. "I remember one of her favorite shows was *Gunsmoke* with James Arness," Donna says. "We never missed that one or any other good cowboy show. She'd talk to the TV and tell them when someone was sneaking up behind them. I would get so tickled at her because she got so caught up in the shows."

Of course, any time two women get together, regardless of their ages, the subject of men is going to come up. It was the same with Donna and Minnie. "I'd tease her about the men there at Graceland. There was a guard named Fred Stowe and I would joke with Dodger about him being her boyfriend," Donna says. "She would laugh and say, 'Hello!' That was her swear word."

When Elvis was at home, Donna got even more of a thrill

out of spending time at Graceland. He always was giving her little gifts and trinkets, she recalls. "I know some people think that we always were up there asking Elvis for things, but that's not true. You didn't have to ask; if Elvis wanted you to have something or thought you needed something, he gave it to you." Obviously, he thought this shy, quiet cousin who was so devoted to Minnie needed these things to make her feel self-confident and bring her out of her shell more.

"Boy, if I had held on to those things, can you imagine? I could pass them on to my sons and grandchildren and say, 'Here's something that Elvis gave me,' " Donna says. Unfortunately, Donna's sister, Susie, sort of wiped out the family treasure chest. "I kept all those things he gave me in a little cigar box," Donna remembers. "One day I couldn't find it and I realized that Susie had locked herself in the bathroom. I went to the bathroom door and said, 'Susie, have you seen my cigar box with the things Elvis gave me?' and she says, 'No, and if they're broken I didn't do it.' That was the end of my Elvis collection."

Not all of Donna's time at Graceland was spent with her grandmother and Elvis. Sometimes, she would go outside and talk to the fans who were milling about Graceland. "Back then, the fans were allowed to walk up to the house — just around the circular drive, nowhere else — and they could take pictures and visit with each other. It gave me a lot of enjoyment to visit with them. A lot of times, I would go out front and take pictures with them and talk to them.

"Often they were from different countries and they didn't know what I was saying. I certainly didn't know what they were saying. But, it's funny, we always managed to communicate with each other. I'd sit and talk for hours with them. I learned a lot about people. I found out it doesn't matter where you're from, what you do, what your social status is, what color you are or anything else. Everybody basically is the same — they have the same needs, same desires, same thoughts."

There was one other person who regularly was a part of the mix at Graceland. Elvis' Aunt Delta, one of Minnie's daughters, came to live in the mansion when her husband died. If Minnie was the solid ground that the family walked on, Delta was the mine field planted there. She was feisty, full of red-headed good humor. She, like the other Presley women, spoke her mind and she did it often. Aunt Delta kept things hopping.

"She pretty much oversaw the running of the household. She took care of seeing that the groceries were all bought, that the maids had anything there they needed to cook," Donna explains. "She made sure that all the buildings at Graceland had locks on them and she kept the keys. She was in charge of seeing to it that the workers could get into the buildings they needed to. She was a lot of help to Elvis and to Uncle Vernon."

One way she tried to help was filling in when one of the cooks was away. Apparently, Delta wasn't the best of cooks. Nash remembered:

> One time she was helping in the kitchen and one of the guys came in and asked who was cooking and Delta said she and Nancy (one of the maids) were. He said, "I'm not hungry."

"The thing I remember the most about Aunt Delta is her wit," Donna says. "She had that dry sense of humor that Uncle Vernon had and she could really keep you laughing. Of course, she did have a temper, too. One thing about Aunt Delta — you never had to guess where you were as far as what she thought of you. She'd just tell you straight out. She didn't care if it hurt your feelings or not. She'd tell you. If it hit Aunt Delta's mind, it would come out her mouth.

"But she was a loving woman. She was real warm and she was kind and generous. She cared about her family."

Aunt Delta, Donna says, "was one of those colorful people. I always got a kick out of her. She was a lot of fun to have around, but she could cause some problems, too. Every now and then, she liked to drink and when she did, she was trouble on wheels.

"She gave Elvis some pretty hot moments because he never knew what she was going to say and she didn't care who it was in front of when she did decide to say it. She put us all on the hot seat at times."

Elvis worried about his public image. He was afraid people would think he didn't take care of his family. It was something that always concerned him and he knew that people who didn't live at Graceland never could understand what life was like inside. Some of his relatives helped him with his image. Others didn't. Nash recalled one of those times:

> One time, Delta and I were in Mom's room and Elvis was in there talking to us. I told him that some lady asked me if Elvis would speak to me. He said, "You should have told her, 'Yes, and if he cuts his arm, it will bleed just like anyone else's.' "
>
> Then Delta said, "Well, I had a lady to ask me if I was allowed in the mansion and I told her, 'Hardly ever.' " (She was living there at the time.) Elvis laughed and said, "Aunt Delta, you're a big help."

Delta liked to wear wigs. It's a wonder she did because those wigs gave her no end of trouble and provided her family a constant source of entertainment. That was one of the reasons that so many of her wigs ended up getting thrown into fires.

Once she was out horseback riding with Elvis and some of his friends and, of course, she had on one of her wigs. Her wig got caught on a tree limb and while she was trying to get it loose, she fell off the horse.

"The wig went one way and she went the other," Donna laughs. "Elvis nearly fell off his horse laughing at her. When he finally did get down off his horse, he still was laughing at her. He was rolling around on the ground laughing. She didn't care, because she thought it was funny too. But later on, she decided it embarrassed her and that made her mad, so she burned the wig. It didn't matter to her about the expense, once she got it into her mind, she was going to do it."

Nash recalled another time when Delta and one of her wigs parted company:

> Delta was going to give one of the maids one of her wigs. Two of them (the maids) wanted it and they started arguing over it, so Delta took the wig out in the backyard and burned it. Elvis came downstairs and saw what was happening. He laughed so hard. He said, "You never know what Aunt Delta is going to do next."

Elvis loved the spice that Delta brought to Graceland. With her there, it was like a powder keg, always threatening to produce a minor explosion somewhere, sometime. Still, he needed an anchor. He found that in Minnie. "Elvis was very close to Grandma," Donna said. "She and the rest of his family kept him grounded. They had that strength and that love that he could rely on."

Elvis admired his grandmother's tough, "I'm not going to be conquered" attitude. His admiration was returned. Minnie often told her other grandchildren that she loved them, "but Elvis and Donnie (Minnie's pet name for Donna) are my picks." Elvis and Donna were allowed to call her Dodger. They were allowed to sit on her bed and put their feet there as well. They were the fairest of the fair in Minnie's universe. They loved her unreservedly and got her complete devotion in return. For Donna, it was a wonderful extra in her life. For Elvis, at times, it was life itself. Nash said of her mother:

> She had a marvelous wit and humor, so she fit right in with Vernon and Elvis and their humorous times together. She always had a way of lifting his (Elvis') spirits when he was down.
> He would go into her room at the foot of the stairs, sit down on her bed (with his shoes on no less). She wouldn't let the rest of us do that. They would laugh

and simply enjoy the fellowship they shared.

Elvis received much comfort from her and many words of wisdom. He really loved Mom and, the times he wanted to unwind, he would go into her room. He talked, she listened. She talked, he listened.

Minnie and Elvis enjoyed the less quiet times as well. He would take her riding on his golf cart, running it at his usual speed — wide open — and bouncing around the hill at Graceland. Nash remembered:

Mom would say, "Son, you better slow down or you're going to throw me out of this thing." He would laugh and say, "Grandma, you're tough, you can take it."

Minnie was one of the few people on earth who knew how to handle Elvis. But she had his complete respect. She was tough and she was honest. That's all he looked for in people. He might not have always taken her advice, but he always sought it out.

Often, he sought out some quiet time as well. Even Elvis needed some absolute solitude every now and then. Nash remembered one of those times:

One afternoon, I went over to Graceland to visit Mom, and Elvis was out in the back yard riding around in a golf cart. It wasn't a motorized one, it was one you had to pedal. He was barefooted, had on his pajamas and his hair was tousled...He said, "I'm just taking advantage of the time to be alone and I decided to get out here and ride."

Now that Elvis was home from the Army and his family settled in this insular environment where even he couldn't completely overcome the influence of Minnie, all seemed well in their universe. Little did they know that other planets — more like asteroids, really — were at the edge of their universe, ready to enter it and throw everything off balance.

These were men who would come between Elvis and his family. They would gravitate around Elvis and they would use every power they had to keep Elvis' family just outside the orbit they established with him. These people wanted family members just far enough away that they couldn't pull Elvis to them. These people wanted to be Elvis' universe. They did everything they could to convince Elvis that he could be the center of their orbit. They would do what he wanted, when he wanted it and how he wanted it done. They weren't as big on telling Elvis the truth as they were on telling him what he wanted to hear.

Elvis' family began to feel their closeness to him slip away as these new people, who would become known as The Memphis Mafia, came on board. "There were so many people in there who didn't want the people who really loved Elvis to be around him, because they were so afraid we might get something they thought they were going to get," Donna says. "It's sad, but it's true."

"I've wanted to say it for years," Susie adds. "I want to say it loud and clear. They didn't want us around Elvis."

Vernon worried about what he saw happening to his son. Elvis was a giver. He remembered times when his family had nothing and he didn't want to see other families like that. He had the money that could fix some of those problems, why not use it to do some good?

Elvis generously gave to local charities. He knew Memphis had been good to him. He was good back to Memphis. He helped people he didn't know. If he read a newspaper story about a child who needed clothes for school or some kind of medical treatment, he sent a check. His mother had been the same way. Of course, she didn't have a lot of money when Elvis was young, but she helped out her neighbors and did everything she could for people who were in trouble. Vernon once told Nash that if Gladys and Elvis had had their way, the family wouldn't have a penny left.

When Vernon tried to remind his son that he had to be careful or he might get taken in by people who asked him for help, Elvis would smile and say, "Daddy, you see their wants. I see their needs."

"Uncle Vernon didn't always approve of what Elvis did and a lot of times he thought people used Elvis for financial gain," Donna says. "I know that he was right. I think there were some people who used Elvis just for what he could give them. I think eventually Elvis knew who they were and he knew when they were using him."

The thing that Elvis might not have realized at first was that the people who surrounded him might not have had his best interest at heart. He didn't notice that the people he saw when he was there with his family were not the same people his family saw when Elvis wasn't in the room.

"I remember I would go in there and I'd see these guys sitting around, all spread out, like, 'Oh, I'm Mr. Big. I'm Mr. Wonderful,' " Donna recalls. "Of course, Elvis wouldn't be in the room."

The men seemed to act that way, Edie says, "because they hung out with Elvis." But they put on that act for the family mostly when Elvis wasn't around. "When Elvis came into a room, it was like E.F. Hutton. Everybody listened."

The men listened to Elvis and tried to anticipate and meet his every need, Donna says. Sometimes, they were so eager to do that, they made themselves look foolish.

"I remember one night in particular. I thought this was so funny. Elvis walked out of the kitchen and into what now is the Jungle Room and all the guys were sitting around like they were Mr. Big. Elvis took out a cigar and said, 'Does anybody have a light?' Fifteen hands jumped up with matches or lighters."

"I remember," Susie laughs, "it looked like a room full of lightning bugs in there."

But eventually, Elvis saw through these "yes men." He may not have figured it out as quickly as his family did, but he figured it out. "Elvis had natural instincts as far as dealing with people. He could read people pretty well," Susie says. "He was a pretty good judge of character. That's a trait that goes through our family. We're not fools, you know. We don't fool easily. That's not to say you can't fool us, but we don't fool easily. And once you've fooled us, you won't do it again."

Many members of Elvis' inner circle wrote books about the singer, publishing them before and after his death. "That's what's so frustrating and makes me so angry about these people," Donna says. "They are writing books and saying how bad Elvis was and how he was on drugs and doing this wrong and that wrong. The funny thing is, if Elvis was doing those things, so were they."

One of them wrote about how he and the others were so concerned and worked so hard to try to get Elvis off drugs.

"They say that they wanted to get Elvis off the drugs, they wanted Elvis not to do this or told him it was a bad idea to do that," Donna says. "That is such a joke. They never tried to stop Elvis from doing anything, especially not if they thought they could get something out of it. They were on drugs, they were drinking alcohol, they were getting into trouble.

"I'm not saying Elvis was a saint, because he wasn't. He made mistakes," she says. "But these people were doing the same things Elvis was doing. Some of them were doing even worse."

In fact, Elvis' family doesn't try to hide the fact that, toward the end of his life, he was using, actually abusing, prescription drugs. "Elvis had a number of health problems. Many of the drugs that were prescribed were drugs he needed for those various problems, but I think there was something else," Donna says. "I think one of the reasons he was taking so many drugs was that he didn't want to feel. He was away from God and he was miserable.

"He had attained everything imaginable except the thing he wanted most — peace of mind. He was powerful financially, powerful professionally, but powerless personally. Without God, everyone is.

"I don't think of Elvis as a victim of his fame. I think he was more a prisoner of it.

"Drugs are a killer. They make you see things in a totally

different way. I think the drugs gave Elvis a sense of power that he didn't feel without them.

"When he started taking them, he got caught in a vicious circle. He'd have to take something to be able to sleep. Then he'd have to take something to wake himself up to be able to go on with the next day. One drug led to another and with him in poor health like he was, it all became too much and overwhelmed him."

Nash recalled how she once broached the subject of drugs with Elvis:

I knew drugs were a touchy subject for him, but I had to ask. He looked down and said, "As you know, I'm on prescription drugs that I have to take all the time for health reasons."

Once when Vernon was in the hospital and they had put him on a new medicine that he didn't want to take, Elvis told them, "Give it to me and I'll take it." Then he laughed. Vernon always questioned the nurses about the medication they brought for him to take. He not only asked about the medication, but asked why certain drugs were being administered to him. And Sandy (Vernon's nurse and fiancee) always was with Vernon to watch out for him.

Elvis had medical books and he studied them. He knew what each drug was for. I doubt that he could be fooled easily where drugs were concerned. Granted, he was on prescription drugs, not street drugs, but he was taking too much and too many.

After their brief talk about drugs, Elvis closed the subject with his aunt. And "when he closed the subject, it was closed as far as he was concerned," Nash said. "He didn't want me to know he was on drugs."

Another insider claimed in his book that Elvis, toward the end of his life, was so out of touch with reality that he believed he could move the stars or clouds with his very thoughts.

"Elvis never thought that," Donna answers. "He would sit outside with the guys around and say, 'See that cloud up there? Watch me move it with my mind. See it moving?' Then he'd wait for their response. He wanted to see how many of them would say they could see the cloud moving just because they thought that's what he wanted to hear. It was like that fairy tale 'The Emperor's New Clothes.' When the whole thing was over, he'd come inside and laugh about the ones who said they saw the cloud move. They weren't fooling him, they were fooling themselves."

No matter who they were fooling, the fact remained that they were at Graceland most of the time and they were driving a wedge between Elvis and the people who loved him and really cared for him. It was disconcerting for his family and they were determined not to let it happen. They knew they still had all of Elvis' love and devotion. They just wanted to be sure no one told Elvis that he didn't have theirs. They weren't waging a battle for his attention or for his belongings. As it turned out, they were fighting for his health, for his very life. They knew from the start that it wasn't going to be an easy battle to win, but they weren't going to be defeated without a whale of a fight.

In the end, it would turn out to be a fight they couldn't win. Elvis was battling his own demons — the responsibilities, the prescription drugs, the illnesses, the aging process. The Mafia still was trying to keep him distant from his family. The people who really cared about him were trying to reach in and pull him back from whatever place his fame had taken him. Elvis withdrew to his room at Graceland. There, he felt, he could be in control. No confusion, no having to do anything. It was a place where he could rest and recharge.

"There were one or two people near him at the end who were taking from him instead of giving to him," Edie says.

"In the later years," Susie recalls, "you didn't see him a lot. Even though no doctor ever has said this, I believe he was suffering from depression. When you're depressed, you isolate yourself because that's the first protective thing you think of to do. You either isolate yourself or you put yourself out there with so many people that you get lost in them."

Elvis seemed to be trying both methods at once. No middle ground. Either he was isolated or he was out in the crowds. It was obvious to his family that he was struggling to balance out what he could do (after all, he was just a human being) and what he thought he had to do.

"You push and push and push yourself," Donna adds, "until there's nothing left to give. That's what Elvis did."

Elvis' family began to feel differently about being at Graceland. It just wasn't quite the same.

"It was like you could feel a black cloud rolling in," Edie says, "and there wasn't a thing you could do about it."

7

"We had a great time and
were great friends."

ONE NEW FACE THAT was welcomed at Graceland was Priscilla's. Elvis had left her behind in Germany, promising to call her often, telling her she meant a great deal to him. At a press conference when he got home, he told reporters their relationship wasn't anything special, that she was just another girl. That may have been what he told the press and it may even have been what he was telling himself. But something inside him wouldn't let him just erase Priscilla from his life.

He did call her in Germany, not often enough to suit Priscilla, and they even talked about her coming to Memphis. After much discussion, negotiation and compromise, Elvis finally convinced her parents to put Priscilla in his care. She would live, he assured them, with Vernon and his new wife, Dee, in their home near Graceland. She would go to a carefully chosen school. She would have a car, clothes, anything she needed. She would maintain her grades and she would earn her high school diploma. Elvis would guarantee that nothing would happen to her. Reluctantly, her parents finally gave in. Priscilla packed her clothes and headed for Tennessee and a new life.

She did live with Vernon and Dee, at least for a little

while. But it wasn't long before her things were making their way to Graceland and she was spending more and more time there. She would go to Immaculate Conception High School during the day, but she would go out on the town with Elvis at night. It was a very strange life, indeed, for a teenager. But it was the life Priscilla had chosen and it was a life that was the envy of almost every other teenager in America.

It wasn't as glamorous as those teenagers might have thought, however. Elvis was gone often, touring or making movies, and Priscilla was at Graceland with Elvis' family. She and Minnie became close. In fact, Priscilla was one of the few people besides Elvis and Donna who was allowed to call her Dodger. Still, the fact was that Priscilla was young and most of the people at Graceland were much older. They weren't really her family. She was separated from the man she loved and there were constant rumors that he was seeing other women.

It couldn't have been easy for Priscilla. She wasn't even out of high school yet and certainly couldn't be considered mature by any standards. At times she lived in a world of her peers and at times she lived surrounded by grown-ups. The only constant she knew was Elvis and every time she picked up a magazine or read a newspaper or saw a television show about him, there was a mention of his latest female co-star. They usually were seen riding motorcycles or partying after hours on the movie set and they always were linked romantically. Finding some sort of solid ground to stand on wasn't easy.

To add to Priscilla's frustrations, she and Elvis were sleeping together, but that literally was all they were doing — sleeping together. It was obvious to her from the things she read and heard that more than that was going on with the other women in Elvis' life, which always left her wondering what she was doing wrong. What she failed to understand was Elvis' upbringing. He was taught to respect the women he loved. He loved Priscilla, and respecting her meant not engaging in sex with her until they were married. His view of respect and sex may have been a bit skewed, but it was his view and he was sticking to it. To give Elvis his due, it must have been difficult for any man to sleep beside this beautiful young woman each night — often with her pleading with him to consummate their relationship — and not go ahead and say, "Why not?"

Donna made regular visits to Graceland during this time and those visits were a welcome relief for Priscilla. Here was someone near her age, someone who would understand how she felt, someone she could have "girl talk" with, someone to whom she could pour out those frustrations.

"I would go down and spend my summer vacations from school at Graceland," Donna recalls. "Two weeks before school would let out, I would head for Memphis. I always was so excited when the time would begin to get close. I would start packing a month before the time for me to leave. I'd have to take my clothes back out of the suitcase to get ready for school."

Originally, Donna's visits were arranged by Elvis so she could keep Minnie company while he traveled. It suited Donna fine. She loved visiting with her grandmother and besides, it was fun to be at Graceland. "At Graceland, the maids did everything for me. All I had to do was ask and they'd get it," she says. "I had a great time. My cousin Patsy (Vester's daughter) and I would go swimming and laugh and talk.

"I felt just like a fairy princess getting to go to Graceland, living there. No dishes, no washing, no room to clean — it was great. Back at home, I had left my brothers and sister with a lot of chores. They didn't appreciate it much, but I enjoyed it.

"I always had a lot of fun at Graceland."

When Donna first started going to Graceland, Elvis was dating Anita Wood. "She was older than me, but she never made me feel like a worrisome teenager," Donna says. "She would take me shopping with her and out to eat. We had a really good time."

There were rumors that Elvis had another girlfriend, one he had left behind in Germany, but then there always were rumors about Elvis and girls. One day, Anita and Donna found out the talk might be more truth than rumor. "Elvis was on the road and she was expecting a phone call from him, so we went upstairs to Elvis' room," Donna remembers. "She was going through his desk, looking for something and she came across a picture of Priscilla.

"She tore the picture in two and then put the pieces back where she had found the picture. I asked her why she tore it up and then didn't throw it away. She said she wanted him to know she had found it and what she thought about it.

"Later that night when Elvis called, she told him about the picture and said she wanted to know what there was between him and Priscilla. They talked for a long time and Elvis sang, 'She's Not You' to Anita over the phone. That helped to alleviate her fears for a while. But, of course, Elvis and Anita broke up and Priscilla came to Graceland."

When Priscilla became Elvis' official new love interest, Donna just accepted her into the family and the two of them became fast friends. As Donna explains, "We had a great time and were great friends.

"We did a lot of things together — you know, things like shopping, going to the movies. Priscilla and I would go out with Jean Boyd, a very close friend of mine. We would go to eat, go to the zoo, to the fairgrounds and ride the rides. I liked the Pipkin, the roller coaster. Priscilla and Jean liked all the rides, the faster and more scary, the better. Priscilla would get up on the Ferris wheel and rock the seat we were in. It always scared me to death, but she got a big kick out of it.

"One night, Priscilla and I went to the fairgrounds and she got me on this rocket thing. It went around and around in a small circle. The centrifugal force knocked you back in the seat and you couldn't move. She loved it. I got deathly ill. I was so sick, I had to lay down in the back seat of her Corvair all the way home. Priscilla thought it was hilarious. I did, too, once I was able to."

The two young ladies also pursued higher matters together. "I belong to the Assembly of God and Priscilla was

Catholic, so we decided to go to church together," Donna says. "One Sunday we went to her church for early Mass. It was very different from anything I was used to, but it was one of the most beautiful services I have ever been in. Everyone is so reverent and, of course, the church is so ornate and impressive. Priscilla really got tickled at me because I thought the kneeler was a foot stool."

When they went to the Whitehaven Assembly of God church together, Priscilla "was enthralled by the service and deeply moved," Donna says. "I remember after the prayer she said it was so moving that she cried."

Priscilla, obviously, was a very attractive young woman. Donna has all the Presley good looks wrapped up in a striking, slim package. The sight of the two of them out exploring Memphis was bound to attract the attention of young men. One of them got up the courage to ask Priscilla to go out with him. "She was very tactful," Donna recalls, "and she didn't want to hurt his feelings. She just told him she couldn't because she was involved with somebody. We laughed and wondered what he would have thought if she had told him who that somebody was."

When the two of them were at Graceland, they spent part of their time just talking about things — school, what movies they liked, make-up, clothes and the normal things that teenagers talk about. It's probably hard for parents to accept and for men to imagine, but sex is another thing that teenage girls talk about. Donna and Priscilla were no different. In front of Minnie, Priscilla said that she and Elvis weren't having sexual relations and that they wouldn't have them until they were married. To Donna, she poured out the frustrations that came with Elvis' decision to have their lives be that way. Priscilla felt that Elvis' physical expression of their love would bind them more closely together and maybe even stop whatever events were engendering the stories of his nights with his co-stars. Besides that, she wanted to be completely in touch with him. She loved him.

If Elvis could see the advantage of having Donna there for Minnie, he certainly could see that it was an advantage to have her there for Priscilla as well. She and Priscilla were growing up together at Graceland and becoming good friends in the process. With her there, everyone was more content.

Elvis asked Nash if Donna could come and live at Graceland. He made her the same promises he'd made to Priscilla's family. She would have anything she wanted, she would get an education and Elvis would provide for and protect her. Nash's answer was different, however. She decided the place for her 15-year-old daughter was at home and she told Elvis so. "She's mine and I need to raise her," she gently explained. Elvis may have been disappointed, but he wasn't offended. He understood about family.

Had Donna been given the choice, of course, her bags would have been packed for Graceland. "I thought it was a great idea. You know, the best schools, new car, new clothes. Anything and everything I could possibly want," she says. "I thought it would be wonderful, but my mom thought better of it. My mom was 15 when she and Daddy got married and Grandma loved my dad very much. But Grandma always teased my mom about getting even with her for running off and getting married by getting me married off when I was 15. Perhaps my mom thought that Grandma really did intend to marry me off."

Looking back at her teenage years, Donna has to confess that her mother might have been right. "It probably was best that I remain at home. But I sure didn't think so at the time. I've looked back at times and wondered what my life would have been like if I had moved to Graceland. I know it would be very different. There would have been a lot of good things about it. But I would have missed growing up with and really getting to know my sister and my brothers. I don't live my life thinking about what might have been. I don't spend it regretting things I might have missed. But sometimes in the back of my mind I think about it."

Elvis' family knew it was inevitable. He and Priscilla would get married. It was just that no one — least of all Elvis and Priscilla — knew when. They did move one step closer on December 25, 1966. Elvis officially proposed to

Priscilla and gave her an engagement ring as a Christmas gift. Even if all of Elvis' female fans were envious of the new role Priscilla played in his life, they were happy for him. Priscilla, they conceded, certainly was beautiful enough to be Elvis' mate and she truly seemed to care for him. Fans were pleased that he had found someone who would make him happy.

The only thing that remained undone was setting the date.

Since this wedding involved Elvis and not many of the things around him took place in a normal style, no one really expected engraved invitations and a big church full of flowers, with Priscilla's friends attending her dressed in various pastel shades. To be sure, the wedding Priscilla had probably was nothing like the one she might have dreamed of when she was a little girl. In fact, at this wedding, the bride wasn't even the center of attention. That spot belonged to the groom.

Without telling very many people at all, Elvis and Priscilla took a few friends and family members and flew from Palm Springs, California, where he was filming a movie, to Las Vegas on May 1, 1967. They got there at 3 a.m. and by 3:30 a.m., they had been issued a marriage license by the Clark County Clerk's office. It cost them $15 to get the license.

At 9:41 a.m., Priscilla Beaulieu became Mrs. Elvis Presley in a double-ring ceremony at the Aladdin Hotel. After most weddings, there's a reception where the bride and groom share a cake and the groomsmen sneak outside to paint on the "getaway" car with shaving cream. After Priscilla and Elvis' wedding, there was a press conference. After the press conference, there was a small reception for some of their close friends. They ended the day back in Palm Springs and Elvis went back to work on his movie.

Donna and her family were living in Missouri at the time that Elvis and Priscilla married. She recalls finding out that her cousin and her great friend were married when she heard the news on a television report. It didn't upset Donna to find out this way. It was the way things were when you were related to Elvis. Life was full of surprises. And this particular surprise pleased her very much.

About three weeks after the much-publicized wedding, Donna's father, Earl Pritchett, went to work for Elvis at Graceland and her family moved to the ranch Elvis had bought in Mississippi. Though it was in another state, the ranch was about 30 miles from Graceland and several of Elvis' friends and employees lived there.

When the movie wrapped in Palm Springs, Elvis and Priscilla arrived at the Circle G Ranch for their official honeymoon. "There was a beautiful house on the ranch," Donna remembers. There also was a red and white mobile home. That's where Elvis and Priscilla spent their honeymoon — and where they stayed when everyone came out to the ranch for weekends of horseback riding — because, "Elvis thought it would be a great experience to live in a mobile home. He thought they were the neatest things in the world," Donna explains.

Elvis' family may have missed out on being at his wedding, but he wasn't going to let them miss out on the celebration. He threw a wedding reception to end all wedding receptions at Graceland when he and Priscilla got back there. Donna remembers it as a magical evening.

"It was great fun and everyone had a wonderful time. Elvis had music and champagne and plenty to eat and drink for everyone (even those like my family who didn't drink alcoholic beverages). Everyone toasted Elvis and Priscilla and then Elvis and Priscilla gave me their glasses to hold while they danced."

Mr. and Mrs. Elvis Presley were officially in residence at Graceland.

8

"She was a free spirit."

JUST AS THERE HAD been excitement in Tupelo, Mississippi, before Elvis and his brother were born, there was a stir at Graceland. Priscilla and Elvis were going to have a baby. The house always was busy, alive, but now it would take on a special life — there would be a new Presley there. Elvis may not have been happy about his movie roles, craving more substance and less fluff, but this was a role he was eager to take on. He was going to be a daddy.

The whole house was on pins and needles, waiting for this new generation to arrive. To understand just how much it meant to all the Presleys, one has to understand about Southern families and babies. At one point in the life of the South, babies were welcomed because each child meant another field hand, someone else to help coax crops from the land that wasn't always cooperative in that regard. In addition to the practical side of adding to the family, there was the emotional side. Blood truly runs thicker than water in the South. To have someone new to carry on the name was not only important, it was expected. Old maid aunts were pitied. The names of young women who found they couldn't have children were whispered and always preceded by "that poor …"

Just because Elvis had left Tupelo, he hadn't left that heritage behind him. Couples were expected to have children when they married. Otherwise, what was the point of getting married anyway? Of course, they weren't necessarily expected to have them quite so quickly. Within days of their wedding, Elvis and Priscilla were expecting a new arrival. In a television interview she did with Barbara Walters years after Elvis' death, Priscilla laughed and said she was sure Lisa Marie was conceived on their wedding night.

There may have been more than a little truth in that. On February 1, 1968, exactly nine months to the day after their wedding, Elvis and Priscilla left Graceland, headed for Baptist Hospital and a new phase of their lives. They got there at 10:40 a.m. At 5:01 p.m., Lisa Marie Presley was born. The newest Presley weighed six pounds, 14 ounces and was 15 inches long.

Delivering a baby isn't always the best thing for a woman's looks. Priscilla knew this and wanted to put on her make-up right after Lisa Marie was born. This was before natural childbirth and Lamaze became popular, so Priscilla had been given an anesthetic that left her a little woozy.

"She told Patsy and me that one of her friends was trying to help her put her make-up on," Donna says. "But Priscilla wasn't happy with the way her friend was doing it, so she grabbed an eye pencil and tried to do it herself."

The problem was, Priscilla told them, that her perception was a little bit off. She kept trying to put the eyeliner on her reflection in the mirror. Of course, she couldn't get it right because every time she moved her head, the eyeliner on the mirror moved to another part of her face.

"She was so out of it because of the medication, she couldn't figure out what the problem was," Donna laughs. "She didn't even realize what she was doing until everybody in the room started laughing and finally explained to her what was going on."

Priscilla got the make-up problems worked out, however, and was looking her best when she and Elvis took Lisa Marie home to Graceland four days later. There, they settled her in her upstairs nursery just down the hall from their room.

"Everyone was excited about Lisa Marie, especially Priscilla and Elvis," Donna remembers. "Of course, Elvis was very nervous, as are all first-time fathers. After she was born, Elvis carried her around on a pillow."

It wasn't long before Graceland was experiencing an onslaught of relatives. It's another Southern tradition. When a new baby is born, everybody in the family comes to see it. It's sort of an official welcome to the family. It's probably one reason Southern babies are so healthy. Within a few weeks, they've been exposed to practically every germ known to man because they've been kissed by every cousin, every aunt and every grandmother they've got. Elvis' family was no exception. They wanted to see his new daughter and he delighted in showing her off.

"He had her name on everything," Edie says. "He had it on one of the golf carts. He had her name on her door. She pretty well had him wrapped around her little finger."

Chubby cheeked, with delicate hands, the little bundle had dark eyes and a tiny nose. Her dark hair — and she had a fair amount — was styled into a "baby curl" on top. The relatives who came to call on the newest family member marveled once again at how so small a package could reduce a grown man to a baby-talking bundle of pride and nerves.

Elvis loved children and especially thought his own was the most wonderful child ever to be born. As much as he carried her around, it was a wonder she ever learned to walk. When Priscilla was pregnant, Elvis might have had a fleeting thought about how nice it would be to have a son to carry on the Presley name, but there was no way on earth he could have been happier with a son than he was with Lisa Marie.

Elvis and Priscilla didn't like to be away from Lisa Marie, but when they had to be, they could count on having plenty of built-in babysitters. Delta was always there and she would recruit visiting cousins to help her with the job. Edie remembers that she was about 16 when she began her babysitting time with Lisa Marie. "Lisa Marie was just an infant," she says. "I remember 'wagging' her around." (In the South, babies are "wagged around" often. Anywhere else in the country, it would be called "carrying the baby around.")

When Lisa was small and not independently mobile, the responsibility was great — you didn't want to let anything happen to Elvis' child. Once she became upright and started moving on her own, the task of supervising her was next to impossible. "Trying to keep up with her," Edie recalls, "was like running after a little jack rabbit."

Most of the family thought she inherited that trait from the Presley side of the family. As Nash said:

> *I told her one time that she was like her daddy.*
> *She knew one speed and that was wide open. She was*
> *a tough little thing and good at everything she tried*
> *to do. I know Lisa was a blessing to Elvis.*

Edie would tell folks that Lisa had "a lot of spit and vinegar in her." When Minnie overheard her once, she asked, "Where did you learn to say that?"

"I told her, 'Grandma Hacker taught me that,' " Edie says. "Now when Minnie and my grandma got together, they did some pretty racy talking sometimes, but Minnie wouldn't let me say 'spit and vinegar.' "

Lisa Marie wasn't "spit and vinegar" to her father. She was a rose. He once told Edie that Lisa Marie was "the brightest rose that was ever brought into my life."

"He said that Lisa Marie was his joy and that one day I would have a child and would understand," Edie remembers.

If Elvis set out to teach his daughter that she was special, he did a good job of it.

As a child, Susie recalls, "Lisa Marie would go up to adults and say, 'Well, my daddy is Elvis Presley. What do you do?' "

The little Princess ruled over Graceland, completely in command of her father and most of the other adults in the house. Nash remembered one time she and Elvis discussed Lisa Marie:

> *We talked about Lisa and the cute things she did and said. He told me she would come upstairs and say, "Daddy, I don't think you're going to like what the maids are cooking for your dinner." Then he would send her back downstairs to straighten things out.*

Naturally, Lisa Marie was indulged beyond any child's wildest dreams. She became a part of everything that went on at Graceland. Her mother and father had horses, so she had a horse, too. Everyone used golf carts to get around the grounds at Graceland, so Lisa Marie got her own golf cart. Nash said:

> *Once Elvis bought her a golf cart, had a canopy put on top, painted it light blue and put her name on the side. She had such a good time driving the other golf carts around, I guess Elvis thought she should have one of her own. She would get some of her friends and they would drive all over the grounds.*

There are certain things that mark changes in one's life. When you're young and unattached, you have a sporty car with room for just two. You live in a wonderful, clean, efficiency apartment. Then you get married and you get a sensible car — one that the wife can drive to the grocery store and have room to bring back more than a loaf of bread in. You move into a one-bedroom apartment and you find that your spouse brought stuff to the marriage, too. Your orderly apartment of the past now becomes a blend of two styles — your post modern and her Victorian.

Before you know it, you're looking at station wagons and ranch houses in the suburbs. A short time later, you're putting a swing set in the back yard and the little woman is inviting the other women over for "baby playtimes."

Elvis and Priscilla skipped the VW bus and the sharing time with parents of other infants, but a swing set did appear in the backyard at Graceland. Even Elvis couldn't escape that inevitable result of fatherhood.

Typical all-American dads put up swing sets, but they don't usually shower their little girls with diamonds and furs before they are old enough to walk. Being anything but typical, Elvis was at the furriers and the jewelry store early on in Lisa Marie's life.

By the time she was four, Lisa Marie had a white fur coat and rings that her father had specially made for her. Not surprisingly, knowing Elvis' love for the flower, one ring was shaped like a rose. Even at that young age, Lisa Marie was developing a taste for things beautiful and sparkly. She loved the rings, though all of them were too big for her. Priscilla, trying to bring some sense of reason to the whole thing and knowing how prone children are to lose anything they have in their hands for more than a few minutes, refused to let Lisa Marie have the rings until she was 18.

And, naturally, Lisa Marie's bedroom would be nothing like you'd expect a four-year-old's bedroom to be. There would be no bunny borders and pink wallpaper in there. Lisa Marie had a yellow bedroom. Among her furniture was a bed so high off the floor that, when she was small, she had to climb up steps to get into it.

The bedroom, with the same bed and the same steps — even though they aren't necessary anymore — still are there in Graceland, just the way they always were. First the room welcomed Lisa Marie when she came home from the hospital. Later it was there for her when she visited her family at Graceland. Today, it's there for her when she comes back to oversee the workings of what has become a major tourist attraction for Memphis and the Southeast.

Being Elvis' daughter, of course, meant pushing the envelope. Elvis raced the golf carts around the grounds. Lisa Marie had to know if hers would go as fast as her father's. Once she found out it would, that was the only speed at which the cart was driven. As Nash recalled:

> *Elvis used to ride through the pasture on the golf carts, go up to Vernon's back gate, go in and visit*

with his daddy. Lisa did the same thing. Sometimes she would go over by herself and sometimes she would take her friends with her. She would drive those golf carts so fast I feared for her and her little friends, too.

After Donna's husband Buddy became part of the security force at Graceland, he became a childcare provider as well. "Part of my job description was to watch after Lisa," he says. "That was no easy task, especially when she would get on the blue golf cart Elvis bought for her. In fact, she took the canopy off the top of the golf cart when she ran in under a low branch on a tree. But she was just like any other girl her age. She was a sweet and fun–loving child and we all loved her."

The swimming pool at Graceland was another natural gathering place for Lisa Marie and her playmates. As Nash recalled, they even tried to teach "Aunt Nash" to swim:

Sometimes, they all would go swimming and Lisa was a good swimmer even back then. If my grandchildren were down there swimming, I would go down and watch them. In fact, all my granddaughters except Kimberly Ann learned to swim in Elvis' pool. They all tried to teach me, but, bless their little hearts and my little heart, I didn't make it. All those children were small and they knew how to swim, but I never did learn.

"When Lisa Marie was a child," Donna remembers, "she was a wildcat. She was a daredevil. She went at everything as fast as she could go. There were times when she wasn't exactly a well-behaved child."

Elvis' devotion to his family and his desire to have them close by meant that Lisa Marie shared one part of her father's growing-up experience. She was surrounded by cousins and seldom at a loss for playmates.

"She was a good kid. She shared with people," Donna says. "She loved to be around other people. They all had a good time. There would be times when she would get in arguments with the other kids — she could be very demanding. But it all straightened itself out in a few minutes and they would all be back playing together just like regular kids all do."

Edie says that Lisa Marie "had no choice but to be beautiful. Elvis was a beautiful man and Priscilla was a beautiful woman. When you see her, you can see the combination of the two into this one body."

Having those good looks and being the child of Elvis and Priscilla had its advantages, but her cousins agree that it brought a lot of responsibility to Lisa Marie as well. "I remember picking her up and kissing her and thinking, 'You just don't know what's going to be ahead of you,' " Edie remembers.

This mixing of Elvis' and Priscilla's genes created something beautiful and something a little magical as well. "She was a free spirit," Edie says. "She still is."

During Lisa Marie's adolescent and teenage years, Priscilla tried to shelter her from much of the publicity — and inherent responsibility — that came with being the daughter of Elvis Presley. And she did as good a job of it as anyone could have. "Elvis always knew that Priscilla was a good mother," Donna says.

Still, Lisa's life would have been different if Elvis had lived, Donna is convinced. "She would have had more time at Graceland. It just seems that California is a different lifestyle and I think he probably wanted to bring her up basically with the same values that he had," she adds.

It wasn't that Priscilla did the wrong things for Lisa Marie, Elvis' family believes, only that Lisa would have had the extra influence of his family and the Southern lifestyle if her father had been alive. It would have created a different Lisa Marie, not necessarily a better one or a worse one, just a different one.

Even during her teenage years, Lisa Marie still came back regularly to Graceland to visit. At a time in their lives when most youngsters would want to be as far as possible from the older members of the family, Lisa Marie seemed to enjoy coming back to the place she knew as home. She liked visiting with her relatives.

"She liked french fries, so the maids would fix her a big plate of them and she'd bring them out to the office and she and Patsy and I would talk," Donna says. "We would talk about different things — whatever she wanted to — her dad, what she was doing, school, boys. She was big into boys. She would tell us who she liked and who she wanted to meet. She was quite a little girl. I remember her saying one time that her favorite performer was Michael Jackson."

Lisa Marie's first marriage — to Danny Keough — produced two heirs to the Graceland throne — Danielle and Benjamin. It also made Priscilla a grandmother, though certainly not your "hair in a bun, 'Hand me my cane, honey' " variety. Fans who still think of Elvis at the age he was when he died would find it hard to believe, but it would have made him a grandfather, too.

It's a role he would have loved, Edie believes. "He loved children, he loved having Lisa Marie. He would have relished the idea of being a grandpa."

Lisa Marie took time out from her role as new mom when her own daughter was born to thank the Elvis fans all over the world who had sent cards, letters and gifts. In fan newsletters, she wrote:

"Dear Friends,

"I've always known that your great love for my father was extended to me. You've always shown so much concern for my happiness and well-being. Now, I feel that love being extended to my husband and child. Danny and I want to thank you for helping us welcome our beautiful Danielle into the world.

"I wish there were some way for me to respond personally to all your cards, letters and gifts, but there are so many that I think my daughter would be in high school by the time I got finished with them! I just want you to know that Danny and I are very happy and that we deeply appreciate your outpouring of love and support. Elvis fans are the greatest. I grew up knowing that."

And what would Elvis have thought about his daughter's somewhat unconventional second marriage? Nash recalled that she and Elvis once had talked about bi-racial marriages:

> *When I asked him about it, he reminded me that one of his employees, who was white, was married to one of his back-up singers, who was black. "There may be problems later on," he said, "but I'm sure they both can handle them."*

Elvis wasn't a man who was racially prejudiced, say Donna and Buddy. He was the sort of person who looked past the outside to what was going on inside people. The fact that Lisa's was a racially mixed marriage wouldn't have been a concern for him, they say.

Donna thinks it must be a concern of some people who talk to her. "When people would ask me what it's like to have Michael Jackson in the family," she said, "I didn't know if they were asking because he's black or because of his unusual lifestyle."

Donna is sure of one thing, however, "I know Elvis loved his daughter completely and that her happiness was his desire," she says. "I don't necessarily think it would have been his desire for her to marry a famous pop star and get into the show business-type world because there are so many pitfalls and rocky roads. He would have wanted to protect her from that. But obviously for a time, Lisa Marie and Michael were happy with their marriage and Elvis would have had the attitude that if that's what she wanted, no one has the right to tell another person who he can love."

Lisa's and Michael's backgrounds may have been what brought them together in the first place, Donna says. "They had a lot of things in common. They were brought up in a fishbowl, so maybe they had a mutual sympathy about that that brought them together.

"They were both so special and hounded by photographers all the time. They couldn't have had a normal child-hood. They would naturally have to have an affinity and a compassion for that. They would have to understand each other. They also had in common that they both survived this kind of childhood.

"They were friends first and some of the best loves are based on friendship. I believe that you have to have a love and a friendship and be able to help each other through the bad times as well as enjoy the good."

Of course, being Elvis' daughter has meant that Lisa Marie, the all-grown-up woman, now nearing 30, has had to make some adjustments in her life. Just as her mother tried to shelter her from the publicity and the cameras, Lisa Marie has tried to see to it that her children, Danielle and Benjamin, haven't had their faces on the front of every tab-loid at the check-out stands. She tries to assure privacy for them. That need for privacy is another thing carried on the DNA of the Presley gene.

Like her father, she finds that cameras follow her wher-ever she goes. She's learned never to leave the house without looking around for photographers. She looks in the trash, in the leaves, everywhere. She can just sense when there are photographers around.

And they always seem to be there. They chase her through airports. They follow her on shopping excursions.

Like her father, she doesn't ask for much out of life. She'd like to find love. She wants to be a good mother. And she wants to raise happy, healthy kids.

What does Elvis' family want for this child who looks even more like her father today than she did when he was bouncing her on his knee? Donna says, "We want her to be happy."

9

"To our family, he was a gift."

"GOING AWAY FROM YOUR raising." It's a Southern expression. If a good Southern Baptist girl, for example, moves to New York, dyes her hair purple, has her tongue pierced and gets the lead role in a nude off-Broadway musical, she has "gone away from her raising."

Despite what it might have seemed like from the outside, "going away from his raising" is something Elvis never did. When someone gets as famous as Elvis did, he might be tempted to sort of gloss over the fact that he was born in a two-room house that didn't have an indoor bathroom. Elvis didn't mind people knowing that. He wore it as a sort of badge of honor.

And, true to his Southern upbringing, when he got to the top, he brought his family with him. They had been there with him when he would have had to reach up to find the bottom. He wasn't going to forget that just because he had been successful. As Nash said:

> *The faster he scaled the ladder of success, the more he wanted to share with his family and friends. It was as if he couldn't enjoy the fruits of his labor if he couldn't take everyone else with him.*

137

Elvis also knew being rich and powerful did not measure the greatness of a man. However, he did know that love, giving, sympathy, caring and forgiving could make a man stand straight and tall, because he didn't have the weight of holding onto everything he possessed.

He's been called the King of Rock and Roll, a title he didn't care for. He said many times that there only was one King and that was Jesus Christ.

He welcomed his family members into his home, gave them jobs at Graceland so they could be near him and entertained them with each new "toy" or interest he acquired. "We never thought of him as being the 'rich cousin' or anything like that," Donna explains. "To us, he was just cousin Elvis, another member of our family. Sure, it was fun to enjoy the things at Graceland, but that wasn't what made us love him. And he was somebody we loved very much."

Elvis, in fact, seemed to be in awe of some of his cousins. When he would introduce Edie to his friends, he would call her "the cousin who's going to college." He would put his arm around her shoulder and beam, "She's going to be the first one in the family to graduate from college."

Elvis seemed to take a special interest in Edie and her career, so much so in fact that it appeared he often wanted to be the guiding force when it came to her personal life as well as her professional one. And Elvis was accustomed to getting his way.

When Edie was 19, she was dating a gospel music singer named Aubrey. Elvis thought she should meet — and date — Cecil Blackwood, one of the Blackwood Brothers. When he mentioned it to Edie, she reminded him that she already was dating someone. "But Elvis wasn't buying into it," she laughs.

He sent Susie and Edie off to a gospel concert in Memphis, then he got on the phone, making sure that his cousins would "just happen to" run into Cecil and Terry Blackwood before the concert. Sure enough, the "chance" encounter took place.

"Cecil asked me if we could go out after the concert," Edie recalls. "And I said, 'I already have plans.' We talked for a while longer, but it was Aubrey who took me home to Graceland that night. Aubrey knew about my talk with Cecil and I think he was hurt.

"Then, when we get back to Graceland, Vernon comes out to meet us and says, 'So, where's Cecil?' Aubrey left not long after that."

Edie met Cecil for breakfast the next morning and launched a dating relationship that lasted a few months. "But I still really liked Aubrey," she explains. "And Nash didn't think Cecil was right for me. She was right. He had been married before and he was looking for someone to be his wife. I wasn't ready for that yet."

So she and Cecil agreed to be "just friends" and went their separate ways. When she told Elvis they weren't dating anymore, she says, "He looked at me and said, 'But he's a Blackwood!'

"To Elvis, being a Blackwood was something wonderful. He saw other entertainers as having as much or more talent than he did and he never lost that childlike awe of people he thought had so much talent."

Nash put it this way:

> He was brought up with love and consideration for his fellow man. He had a deep love for God and for his family. Even though he was considered the best in his field of entertaining, he never forgot his humble beginnings...
>
> All he asked for was love, loyalty and friendship. He gave and gave and gave and pushed himself beyond endurance while he created a lifestyle of luxury and comfort for those he cared for.
>
> I've gone over to the house to tell him goodbye many times as he was about to leave on tour and I would say, "Elvis, I wish you didn't have to leave." And he would respond, "I do, too, Aunt Nash, but there are too many people depending on me." Elvis

felt the need to take care of all of us.

In spite of all the bad things that have been said about this complex individual, there was something so basically good about Elvis. He had such a yearning in his heart to make life easier for others and he did exactly that. I heard him say on several occasions, "Don't talk about a man until you've walked a mile in his moccasins."

One thing I do know, once you met this man, your life was never the same. Just seeing the way he was toward others challenged you to be a better person than you were the day before.

He was a unique person, a deep thinker with a ball of laughter inside him that rolled around and came out in a thundering laugh that made everyone laugh with him.

He was a bundle of energy, a man who could look past your eyes to the inside of you and read your emotions, feel your hurt and your heartbeat.

To our family, he was a gift.

Elvis did have to undergo some changes as he became more famous. It wasn't easy for him always. When you grew up in the South at the time Elvis did, you grew up trusting people. You lived in a close-knit community where you knew practically everyone and your family had known their families for generations. It was hard, Donna says, for Elvis to give up that trusting nature. It was difficult for Elvis to go from being a very private man, surrounded by just his family and close friends, to being a very public man, surrounded by fans and bodyguards, cameras and tape recorders. "Learning that he couldn't trust everyone was hard for him to do. Uncle Vernon tried to help him do that, but it still came hard for him," she says.

In addition to being very trusting, Elvis, Susie says, was an honest man. Honesty, she feels, is a family trait. "We're just straightforward people and we don't put on airs. We don't try to be something that we're not and I think that's important. We're just who we are." Elvis also learned to temper that raw honesty with wisdom when the occasion called for it, she says. "He couldn't just blurt things out, especially not with the people that Elvis was dealing with. When he first started, he wasn't adept at dealing with people like that. But it's something he learned and cultivated as time went on."

To Donna, one of Elvis' most endearing qualities was his ability to be "in tune with the thoughts and feelings" of the people with whom he came in contact. "I have many happy and precious memories of time I spent with Elvis, but I guess the one that stands uppermost in my mind is when I was 18 years old," she recalls. "I still was living at home with my parents and younger sister and they had gone out of town for a few days. Grandma wanted me to stay with her while they were gone. Grandma was like that. She felt it wasn't safe for a young girl to stay alone.

"Anyway, I was alone in Grandma's room watching television when Elvis came in and sat down. I was very shy and sometimes uncomfortable with other people. Elvis sensed this because he was sensitive to other people's feelings. He was such a caring and compassionate man.

"He came over and sat down on the floor in front of me and crossed his legs, yoga style. He looked up and smiled and then he said something to me I'll never forget. He said, 'You always did have the prettiest blue eyes I've ever seen. You have grown from a pretty little girl into a beautiful young woman. Always remember, you can be and do anything you want to. Never forget that and if you ever need my help, I'll always be there for you.'

"I'm sure Elvis probably was just being kind and loving, the way he always was, but I thought to myself, 'My goodness, here Elvis is probably the most famous person there is right now and he told me I was beautiful. He is surrounded by beautiful starlets and has a beautiful wife and yet he told me I was beautiful.'

"I'll never forget that little talk, because it changed my whole attitude about myself. His words gave me confidence and insight into myself that I had never known before.

"God gave the world a song and a smile when he gave us Elvis."

Elvis constantly told his family that the talent he had was God-given. He knew he was destined to achieve the things he did, he told them, because he had had too many occasions of being in the right place at the right time. "He knew that other people had as much talent as he did," Donna says. "He just felt he was blessed that he was able to be a success with his."

Elvis loved having his family caught up in the whirl of his life. He enjoyed sharing with them. He didn't want to be the only one riding the golf carts or setting off fireworks. He wanted everyone to be either participating or watching. He could buy the things he wanted, go the places he wanted and he felt his family should share in it all. Life at Graceland sometimes could take on the aspects of a three-ring circus with Elvis sometimes playing the ringmaster and more than once taking the role of the head clown. That childlike quality was one of the things about Elvis that Nash especially loved:

> We each have a little boy or girl inside us and I, for one, hope we never lose that person. When Elvis smiled at you, you could see the little boy all tucked inside this man who graced many a stage all over America and brought happiness and good will to many lives around the world.

As everyone acknowledges, "normal" at Graceland was very different from "normal" anywhere else. As Nash said, "I really believe Elvis enjoyed life to the fullest, as far as having fun. He liked to play tricks on people, especially the guys who worked for him, and you never knew what he was going to do."

When Elvis bought a horse for Priscilla, he immediately saw how much she enjoyed riding it. Before long, the stables at Graceland were full. Elvis got himself a horse — Rising

Sun — and quickly became quite the horseman. Naturally, he wanted to share his pleasure with Minnie. She had to see his horse. Now, she could have just looked at Sun through the windows at Graceland, but that wasn't good enough for Elvis. She had to see Sun up close. Instead of taking Minnie to Sun, Elvis brought Sun to Minnie. Nash recalled:

> *...He rode Sun up to the window and he ended up taking him into the house because he wanted Mom to see him. Sun, being a horse, didn't know that Graceland wasn't his private bathroom. You can guess what he did.*

So that more of his family and friends could ride with him, Elvis bought a ranch in Mississippi not far from Memphis and filled it with horses for the whole gang. The man he bought the ranch from had named it Twinkletown Farms. That wasn't exactly the kind of name that Elvis could live with, so within a matter of days, Elvis' family and staff were spending time riding at the Circle G Ranch.

Ordinary days were extravagant at Graceland and the Circle G; holidays were almost indescribable. On every major holiday that traditionally featured fireworks, Graceland became "fireworks central." It would start out with the usual things, sending up bottle rockets and Roman candles and the like. Elvis wanted everyone to watch, so there were plenty of "oohs" and "ahhs" as the skies above Graceland filled with colored lights. As soon as the ordinary got boring, it was on to other pursuits, such as fireworks battles. By this time, the women usually had retreated to the inside to let the guys fight it out. Teams were chosen and lines were drawn. The object, it seemed, was to shoot as many fireworks as possible at the other team. There were few, if any, rules.

If there was something in the way, it became the victim of the attack. Since the mansion often was the thing in the way, it's something of a miracle that there's a house left to tour. "They did catch the back of the mansion on fire one time," Nash said. When the firemen came, Donna remembers, "they told Elvis to be careful, that he didn't want to set the house on fire again. He just laughed and walked out to the fire truck with them." As she points out, "Elvis was a bit of a dare-devil." And Susie adds, "He went where angels fear to tread."

During another fireworks fight, Earl was the thing that got in the way and his new jacket became the spoils of war as it caught on fire and burned. "It was right after Christmas and Elvis shot Daddy with a Roman candle and the coat burned right off of him," Donna says. Nash was philosophical about the whole thing, saying, "I didn't like the jacket anyway."

"When I think back on it now, I can't believe they did those things," Donna says. "I mean they would shoot Roman candles at each other. It was dangerous. I guess we just didn't look at it that way then. Anyway, once Elvis made up his mind to do something, there was no stopping him."

Christmas always was a special time at Graceland, according to Nash. She remembered:

> *It wasn't just the gifts, although everyone likes to receive gifts. It was the excitement, the joy of each one being there and seeing everyone having a Christmas spirit about them — happy, enjoying seeing one another, wishing each other a Merry Christmas.*
>
> *Delta and I had such a good time shopping for Christmas gifts, but the hardest job we had was trying to figure out what to buy for Vernon, Elvis and our mom. They all seemed to have everything they ever needed or wanted, but they always appreciated their gifts.*
>
> *The mansion was decorated so pretty and my husband and a co-worker always went down to Mississippi and got a large, live tree for the dining room.*
>
> *In California, Elvis had seen a driveway lined with blue lights and decided he wanted his driveway lined with blue lights. And he wanted to have different colored lights at the bases of all the trees in the*

This photo was made while Elvis was on leave from the Army.

Elvis' father watches him perform.

Vernon; his second wife, Dee; Elvis' longtime girlfriend, Linda
Thompson, and Elvis at a karate demonstration.

Elvis during a trip to Washington, D.C.

Elvis in one of his favorite situations--
surrounded by fans.

Elvis gets a shoeshine while on leave in Paris. (Courtesy of Daniella Pequiot.)

Elvis and members of his platoon on duty in Germany. (Photo by Elvis' Army sergeant in Germany.)

Elvis takes a break from Army routine. (Courtesy of Polly Childs.)

Elvis and an Army buddy in Germany. (Photo by Elvis' Army sergeant in Germany.)

The family dining room at Graceland. It had this decor when Priscilla and Elvis were married. After Elvis' death, the decor was restored.

Elvis, his grandmother Dodger and Priscilla on the porch at Graceland.

Priscilla, Dodger and Elvis with the family's pride and joy, Lisa Marie.

Donna, Elvis and Susie at Graceland.

The Pritchett Family (Susie, Donna, Earl and Nash)
in the den of Vernon's home in back of Graceland.

The family poses for photos at wedding reception for Vernon Presley and Dee Stanley.

Vernon and Dee's house on Dolan Drive, behind Graceland.

Vernon and his mother, Dodger, in Dodger's room at Graceland.

Lisa Marie and a friend in Lisa Marie's golf cart.

Earl and Rising Sun, Elvis' horse.

Edie at age 4 with 2-year-old
brother David.

Edie and Nash in 1976 at fence in back of Graceland, where family shared many secrets.

Elvis' Aunt Delta and Edmond I pose for a formal portait.

Dodger, in her big chair, and Gary Peppers, a close friend of Elvis.

Elvis' Uncle Vester in his guard uniform at the gates of Graceland.

Earl in front of Graceland's famous gates.

Delta walks Edmond II on the grounds of Graceland.

Nash on the grounds of Graceland.

Nash with Elvis fan Stella Walton.

Nash speaking to a convention of Elvis fans at the Circle G Ranch.

Nash and Charlie Hodge, Elvis' righthand man.

Joining in the singing of "How Great Thou Art"--James Blackwood, Hovie
Lister, Elvis Presley and J.D. Sumner. This photo was taken backstage during a
gospel quartet convention at Ellis Auditorium in Memphis, Tennessee.
(Courtesy of James Blackwood.)

Nash and Susie, seated, with
Donna and Edie.

The Blackwood Brothers, one of Elvis'
favorite gospel singing groups.

Edie, second from left, with siblings Terry, Kim, Phillip and David. This was Christmas 1972, three months before David's death.

The Early Family--Buddy, Jamie, Stacy and Donna.

Edie's wedding day, 1975. From left, her parents, Guy and Sue Blackburn, Edie, her sister, Kim, and brothers, Terry and Phillip.

Edie just before leaving on the *Lisa Marie* for a New York shopping trip.

Even when he was this young, Elvis was wearing his signature belts.

*front yard. The house was outlined in blue lights and
there were Christmas trees right in front of the house,
one on either side of the steps.*

*Then to finish off the theme of Christmas and to
show what Christmas really is celebrated for, a large
Nativity scene was put out in the front under the trees.
It all looked like a fantasyland.*

*On Christmas Eve, everyone gathered around
the dining room table to exchange gifts. Elvis used to
buy gift certificates at Goldsmith's department store
and give them plus his gift. Sometimes he would give
out gift certificates from a local fast-food restaurant
as a joke before he gave out the real gifts.*

To add to the excitement that just naturally went with
being at Graceland, there were the many methods of transportation that Elvis liked to employ while traveling all over
the hill. There was a fleet of motorized golf carts at Graceland.
They were used for ordinary things, like getting from one
part of the acreage to another. And they were used for less
ordinary things, such as racing around the hill, eliciting
screams from both passengers and pedestrians who might
be in the vicinity.

There were go-carts, perfect for speeding up and around
the driveway at Graceland. A 1996 television program featured some home movies of Elvis, made early in his career
when he spent a summer in Biloxi, Mississippi. The tabloid
style show managed to take about 15 minutes of film and
stretch it over four days of programming. After the first in-
stallment, the host of the show teased viewers by saying,
"Tomorrow you're going to see Elvis doing a stunt that could
have cost him his career." When the audience tuned in the
next day, they saw Elvis holding a cigarette paper at arm's
length while one of his friends shot at the paper with a BB-
gun. If the writers on the show considered that career-threat-
ening, they would have loved to have film of Elvis as he put
the go-cart through its paces. Even Minnie, who had a high
tolerance for Elvis' shenanigans, had to leave during some

of those outings. Nash recalled:

> *Sometimes I would go over and sit on the front porch at Graceland with Mom and Delta. We would talk and laugh and have so much fun. Elvis and some of the boys would go out on the driveway and ride the go-carts around the front of the house and down the hill. They went up and down the hill so fast, it's a good thing the go-carts were low to the ground because I don't think they could have made it as fast as they were driving.*
>
> *Mom would say, "That boy is going to kill himself and I don't think I can sit here and watch him."* *And we would go into the house.*

Go-carts and golf carts weren't enough for Elvis. He came up with even more daring vehicles to ride around Graceland. He bought snowmobiles and had them fixed up so they could be ridden in the dirt. He and his friends now had a new way to get around and get around they did. Nash told this story about Elvis, the guys and the garden she and Earl had near their trailer at Graceland:

> *They rode them (the snowmobiles) in the yard and one night after my husband had gone to bed, I heard all the gang out back hollering and having a great time. I looked out the window and there they were, riding up and down our garden, tearing it to pieces.*

That sort of thing happened a lot at Graceland. Elvis' family learned not only to accept it, but to expect it any time he was at the wheel of a vehicle. They took it all in stride and tried to look on the bright side of things. As Nash said:

> *I went to the bedroom and woke Earl and told him he didn't have to worry about weeding the garden anymore because we no longer had one.*

That was the beauty of being Elvis. You just had fun and then repaired the damage. If his parents' financial situation had meant that he didn't have the best toys when he was small, it didn't matter, he was making up for it now many times over. If he and the guys tired of riding outside, they could go inside and race slot cars. If the slot cars got old, there was the pool table. "Elvis shot a pretty good stick," Susie says. "Eight ball and rotation were his favorite games." If they got bored with one thing, there always was something else to take its place.

And there were the big cars. Cadillacs, Lincolns, whatever suited Elvis on the day he went shopping. He bought them by the fleet for his friends, his family members. He gave them out the way some folks hand out bubble gum. He didn't have to do it, but he loved the fact that he could do it.

Susie got her first car from Elvis. It was a Mustang that had belonged to the wife of George Klein, one of Elvis' good friends. She had gotten a new car and Elvis bought the Mustang to celebrate Susie's 16th birthday and the fact that she now could drive.

As Susie remembers, "I had seen the car when my mom and I were at Graceland. It was a classic car, maroon with a beige interior. And I said, 'That's a neat car, I'd like to have that.' So somebody came up and gave me a little, bitty card and I thought, 'Well, that's that. That's all I get.' It was a little card and it had the name of the car on it and Elvis said, 'That's your car...come on out and look at it.' He said, 'You just be careful with it and when you get older, I'll buy you a newer car.' I was shocked."

About that time, Susie's parents came out of Graceland and she showed them her birthday gift. Nash told her to be sure and thank Elvis for the car. "He looked at me," Nash remembered, and said, 'She already has.' "

Susie did try to take good care of the car, but it had its share of bumps and bruises, at least one of them due to the presence of Elvis. "I had one friend come up to see me and she was driving my car, bless its heart, and there was this black car behind us. Elvis was either driving it or had been driving it and she saw him walking around and she backed my car smack into that car, just as pretty as you please. She got out and said, 'Susie, move over here' and she had me sitting in the driver's seat. She went around to the other side. I said, 'Girl, I didn't run into that car. You did.' ''

Based on one of Elvis' driving experiences, he might not have cared who actually was driving when the accident occurred. Donna says that sometimes people found out the hard way not to tell Elvis he shouldn't do something. "Elvis was driving a car that belonged to one of his employees," she says.

"Well, they got back to Graceland after dark and Elvis drove up to the back gate. Only the person who was supposed to be on duty there to let Elvis in wasn't there. So Elvis just threw the car in reverse and backed up a bit. About that time, the man realized what was about to happen. He said, 'Elvis, man, don't run my new car into that gate.' And that was all it took. Elvis threw it into gear and floored it. They went flying through the gate."

Donna's father, Earl, picks up the story:

"A bunch of the guys were standing around outside and one of them says, 'Boy, I'm glad he didn't do that to my car.' So Elvis just throws the employee's car in reverse and rams into the front of that guy's car."

"Of course," Donna says, "Elvis had both cars fixed. He probably would have replaced the one he drove through the gate, but the next day, the employee was going around town bragging about how Elvis had wrecked his new car and was going to buy him another one. Elvis didn't like being taken for granted like that, so instead of buying him a new car, he just fixed the old one."

As much as he disliked being taken for granted, Elvis disliked envy. He saw no point in its existing among his family and friends. He willingly shared his wealth and gave them all the things they needed. There wasn't any reason for one of them to want something another one had. Elvis practiced generosity and liked to see other people do the same thing.

"One time when the driveway was lined with cars and

Elvis was out there talking," Donna remembers, "he saw my dad looking at the new Lincoln one of the guys had received. Daddy opens the car door and says, 'That's really, really nice. I'm really proud for you. That's great. It's a beautiful car.' Elvis overheard him saying that. He was so pleased by the fact that my dad was not jealous, he went out and bought my dad a car. He wanted him to have one, too, because he could just be happy that someone else had such a nice car and he never asked Elvis for one or expected him to get one for him.

"That's the kind of thing Elvis appreciated in people. It wasn't what you could give him or what he could give you. It was just the fact that you loved him and you were happy yourself and happy for others. That's the Elvis I knew and remember."

Elvis, who felt a great responsibility for all of his family members, often handed out advice as freely as he handed out cars. He had learned something from the years he had lived and he thought others should benefit from some of the things he had experienced. Donna recalls a talk she and Elvis had about her life.

"He knew how shy I was and how I felt pretty much like an ugly duckling," she says. "I had no self-confidence. Elvis told me, 'You're intelligent and you've got so much to offer life.' "

"He said, 'Go out and experience life, do what you want to do and don't let anyone or anything hold you down because you can accomplish whatever you want to. If you don't believe it, just look at me. Who would ever have thought that I'd be where I am today?'

"That impacted my whole life. In that brief conversation, Elvis made me feel as though I was the only person in the world at that particular moment. He had that effect on everyone. He really and truly cared about people and he had such an insight into how people were feeling and thinking."

Sometimes, Edie says, he knew other people better than he knew himself. The week before her 1975 wedding, Edie brought her bridesmaids to Graceland as a treat for them.

"Elvis told me I was making a mistake to get married," she says. "He asked me, 'Are you in love with this man?' I told him I was and then we talked for a little while longer. He said that I belonged in the theater. He tried to encourage me. He was great at that, giving advice to other people. He couldn't always see things so clearly in himself, though.

"Finally, he told me, 'You're looking for your brother.' He was right. David had been dead only 18 months. I was on the rebound. I was marrying someone I thought would be like David. I wasn't emotionally a real stable person."

The next weekend, when Nash and Susie (who was a bridesmaid in the wedding) arrived for the ceremony, Edie recalls that she noticed Nash praying a lot. "During the wedding rehearsal, I started crying. I didn't really know why I was crying, but I couldn't seem to stop," she says. "After we got home that night, Nash came into my room and said, 'Edie, God has spoken to me. You cannot marry this man...Great sorrow will come to you.' "

No one could convince Edie to change her mind, though, and the wedding went on as scheduled. At the reception, Nash told her, "I'm really going to pray for you."

"Nash encouraged me to stay in the marriage and I did for 15 years," Edie says. "I thought about what Elvis had said a lot in the first year after my divorce."

Elvis also had a hand in directing Donna's love life. When she was 18 years old, she thought she had found "Mr. Right" and was engaged to marry the young man. "The guy I was engaged to was a demanding type person. I guess you could say he almost was tyrannical. Everything had to be done his way, his time and the way he wanted it.

"I took him over to meet Elvis and Elvis, just like he always did, was talking to him, trying to make him feel comfortable. He asked him, 'Well, when are you and Donna getting married?' And the guy made a dumb remark. He said, 'When she can support me in the style to which I've grown accustomed.' He thought it was funny and I think he felt like he was being funny in front of Elvis.

"But Elvis didn't take it kindly at all. As a matter of fact, the next day when I went to visit, Grandma told me that Elvis had been up all night, fuming about what the guy had said. He kept telling Grandma, 'I will not allow her to be treated that way.' She said Elvis said he wanted to mop the floor with the boy's head because of the way he acted and the way he talked. I didn't feel this way at the time, but I kind of wish I'd let him now."

Donna ended the relationship with that suitor, but she did eventually get married and have two sons. Not long after the first one, Stacy, was born, she took him to Graceland to show him off. The baby was lying on Minnie's bed when Elvis came in to see him. (Minnie's dispensation allowing Elvis and Donna to be the only people to get on her bed extended to their children as well.) "I had just taken Stacy to have some pictures made and I had this little hat on him. Stacy's hair stuck straight up.

"When Elvis picked him up, his hat fell off and Elvis just rolled. He just fell in love with Stacy. He kept saying, 'Look at this baby's hair, it sticks straight up!' He was sitting there, holding him and playing with him and he was calling him 'Little Elmer Fudd.'

"He would kiss him on the back of his neck, you know the little indentation on the back of a baby's neck. He just kept on playing with him and then he said, 'What's his name?'

"I said, 'Stacy Aaron' and he just stopped dead in his tracks. He said, 'Aaron, that's my name.' I said, 'I know, Elvis. I named him after you.' I wish you could have seen the look on his face. It was so full of love and joy. He was like a little kid. Like I had given him a prize. He was thrilled to death.

"He said, 'Well, I tell you what, Stacy, you never have to worry about anything. Cousin Elvis will be here to take care of you. When you get a little bit older, you come here and see me for a job.' Of course, Stacy didn't get to enjoy knowing Elvis that well because Elvis died when Stacy was a small child."

As tender as Elvis could be when he was with a small child or talking to someone he loved, he also had a temper. It is, his cousins admit, a family trait. As one woman he dated put it, "He could hate as passionately as he loved."

Priscilla saw "the real Elvis" as generous, wonderful and considerate. His temper, she discovered, resulted from bursts of frustration.

As Nash put it:

> *I always felt that Elvis handled most situations very well and many times under unusual circumstances. He was an impulsive person and sometimes he would do things on the spur of the moment — many times to his sorrow. He was big enough to apologize to anyone he had offended.*

Elvis' temper was like a summer storm, it built and built then let itself out in lightning flashes of fury. After a few minutes, it exhausted itself and was past. Sometimes, though, during those angry moments, he would do things that were senseless and destructive — basically stupid. As soon as the anger was gone, though, Elvis' sense of humor let him realize how stupid he had been and laugh at himself.

Donna's husband Buddy tells the story of one television set that Elvis destroyed:

"Elvis had white television sets throughout the mansion. They all were marked 'Made for Elvis Presley by RCA.' So one day, he calls up Earl and says, 'Come get this TV, it isn't working right.' Earl told him, 'It's probably just the reception. I've got one just like it and I have problems getting it to work right if the weather is bad.' But Elvis says, 'Well, come up here and look at it anyway.' So Earl goes up to the room and there sits Elvis and the television. Elvis points to it and says, 'Uncle Earl, your television like this, does it have a bullet hole in it like mine does?'"

Because much has been written about Elvis' fits of temper and other less flattering parts of his personality, the things that really were important to him sometimes don't come to the fore. For example, some people who have written about Elvis have intimated that education wasn't important to him. His family members say it was. He always was reading, they say. "He always had a thirst for knowledge," Donna points out.

Because his Aunt Nash had such a knowledge of religion and the Bible, Elvis often sought her out to discuss something he had heard or a passage he had read. Sometimes, it was to talk about his thoughts on how a certain Bible verse might be interpreted. Whatever he wanted to discuss, Nash found that he had given it a lot of deep thought:

> He always was learning. He had a searching mind. And the things he learned through his reading, he wanted to teach others.
>
> The times I had with Elvis were quality times. We discussed the Lord and the Bible. He really liked to talk about the Bible. He was well-versed in the Scriptures.
>
> I guess the times I enjoyed talking to him most were when he got serious and talked about God and how important He was to his life.
>
> He and I discussed the Bible many times. He read the Bible. He was knowledgeable in the Word and he believed what he read. He was a good man, but he knew just being good wasn't enough. He knew the more knowledge you have, the more is expected of you. He really had a strong faith in God.

"Elvis' faith was important to him," Donna says. "He was raised knowing God. If you'll notice when Elvis was singing gospel music you could tell he was singing it from the heart. Sometimes he would cry because he was so moved by a gospel song. He knew the power of God and he knew the Bible very well."

Being so well-read and so curious, Elvis formed his own, very definite, opinions about a lot of things. He and Nash once discussed abortion:

> "Aunt Nash," he said, "there never is a cut-and-dried answer to any situation, because there are so

many extenuating circumstances. I don't think you should take anything you can't give back and only God can give back a life. But, you take a young girl who has gotten pregnant and she's afraid to tell her parents or she does tell her parents and through their shock and hurt they make her leave their home and she feels destitute and is vulnerable to anyone who comes along and offers her a way out. If our daughter, Lisa, should ever be in trouble, I hope and pray she will come to us for help. We both have a strong love for our little girl.

"But, to answer your question, I know abortion is wrong. There always is a better way. It's just finding someone to help you find that better way."

Elvis liked to discuss all sorts of subjects with his family and friends. But when he didn't want to talk about something anymore or if the subject hit too close to home, he either would just stop talking or else make a joke about the subject.

Joking was the way he dealt with talking about getting older. Nash related a story about Elvis and age:

Elvis had his share of pride in himself, as most people do.

One day, Richard Davis (one of Elvis' friends) and I were talking about Elvis and were discussing Elvis' 50th birthday. I asked Richard how he thought Elvis would handle being 50 years of age. Richard said, "His way." I had to admit he probably was right.

Richard said that one night, Elvis and his friends were sitting around talking about what they would do when Elvis turned 50. The guys told Elvis that they would bring a rocking chair on stage for him and he could sit there and sing, "My Way."

Richard said they all got up and bent over and started walking around the room like they were old, pretending to have walking canes. What those guys didn't realize is that people are very young at 50.

Just because he had his own opinions didn't mean Elvis expected everyone else to share them. In fact, he once said that influencing people that way might be too big a responsibility.

"Elvis had his own beliefs and his own faults, but he did not ever want to push his ideas or feelings on to another person," Donna says. "One time we were talking about how a lot of the stars come out and get behind a candidate and try to get other people to vote for him because that's who they are going to vote for. I said, 'Elvis, has there ever been a time when you wanted to come out for a candidate and support him openly?' He said, 'Oh, no, no. I wouldn't get involved in politics that way. I would never want someone to vote for somebody or someone to make a decision that affects as many lives as that would based on what Elvis Presley thought. I want them to make their own decisions about that.' "

Traveling as much as Elvis did and meeting so many different people led him to a natural curiosity about many things, Donna says. He always had a book of some kind nearby. Many of the pictures that were snapped of him boarding and leaving his plane, the *Lisa Marie*, show him with a book in his hand. He always kept the latest volume he was reading with him. It helped pass the hours and it helped occupy a mind that always was wanting to learn one more thing.

One thing that seemed to fascinate him, perhaps because his mother died at an early age, was death. He wanted to know about death itself and what occurred after death and about what happens to the body during death, Donna says.

It doesn't seem to be all that odd a thing to wonder about, she adds. "A lot of people are interested in that. If they weren't, we wouldn't have coroners or funeral directors."

And it's another natural outgrowth of his Southern upbringing, she says. "A lot of times in the South, it was the ladies from the church who came in and cleaned up the body and readied it for viewing. There might have been children running around while this was going on. Death was just a part of life. You didn't go to the funeral home to view the body. The body was brought back to the house. Children in the South were very much exposed to this process of death and were naturally very curious about it. It's a product of growing up in an extended family as well. Perhaps he was more fascinated because he was so bright."

Elvis, she says, just saw everything in a different perspective. "He was very creative and creative people have a different outlook on things. If you've ever studied about great artists and composers, you see that they were different from most of the people of their time. Elvis was different in a lot of ways. He saw things in a totally different light. That's why he was so creative."

Along with the reading there went an enjoyment of quiet games. Nash said:

> He used to play Yatzee, especially when they traveled on the tour bus. One man asked me what Elvis' Yatzee score was. I said, "I don't know, but I'm sure he tried to win."

That competitive spirit carried over to everything he did — from touch football to slot car racing. It accounted for his drive and his determination not to quit. Nash explained:

> He was a big sports fan and he liked to watch football on television. He also liked to play football and even had his own team — made up of friends and employees — for a while. He liked to play racquetball and other games. And he played to win.

"Elvis was a complex person," Donna says. "It sometimes was hard to understand him. But he always knew his family loved him."

10

"Bring me something from Graceland."

BEING RELATED TO ELVIS Presley certainly had its advantages. The good times at Graceland added something to the lives of the members of Elvis' family. And getting a new car when you least expected one or receiving some other wonderful gift had to make the life of a Presley relative look glamorous. In fact, the life of a Presley relative could be glamorous, but there was another side as well.

Everything you said or did was always up for inspection. It didn't take long for you to learn that if you were a member of Elvis' family. From the day you were born, you were a Presley. That meant you represented every other Presley and you didn't want to mess up in that regard. Most children in the South know the expression, "Act like somebody." It means that you don't misbehave when you're out in public — or at home, for that matter. You are a somebody and you are expected to behave as if you are one. Furthermore, you're the reflection of all the somebodies who raised you and you are taught from the start that you don't want to embarrass those people who worked so hard to see to it that you did know how to behave. In the case of Elvis' family, they were a reflection of their mothers and fathers, their grandparents, their aunts and uncles **and** Elvis. He had come a long way

173

from that shack in Tupelo. It was your job to see to it that people didn't think it was a mistake for him to make the journey — and to bring his family along.

It was a matter of adjusting to what was normal for your family. Donna always says that her life was anything but normal by other people's standards. But by Elvis' family's standards, it was run–of–the–mill. Finding yourself surrounded by fans or discovering someone just visiting in your front yard was a part of everyday life. Being approached by fans — anytime, anywhere — was the way life went.

Sometimes, it wasn't easy. In fact, it was easier, really, just not to start out telling people you were related to Elvis. "Half of them wouldn't believe you and the other half would think you were bragging," Donna laughs. "If anybody found out I was Elvis' first cousin, it was because someone else told them. Not me." Her son Jamie says it still is hard to tell people he's related to Elvis. It's not that he's ashamed, it's just that it opens up too many possibilities. Will they believe you? If they do, will they try to use you? "A friendship or a relationship has to go pretty far before I feel comfortable telling them," he says.

Inevitably, people will find out, however. Donna found that the moment of discovery is when the strange requests begin. "I went to school one day — I was a young teenager," she remembers, "and I was sitting in the lunchroom. I was sitting there at this little table with some of my friends. I promise you, this girl brought me a milk carton and asked me to touch it because I was 'of Elvis' blood,' I was related to him. I had been close to him. I had touched him and she wanted me to touch her milk carton. So I touched it. She asked. Why not?"

Donna also remembers that people always wanted to "just touch me" so they could say they had touched someone who had touched Elvis. "And there was this one guy who wanted to play his guitar for me. He thought he sounded like Elvis. I let him play for me, but what could I say? No one sounded like Elvis but Elvis."

Presleys always were being inspected, said Nash:

We always were on display. Sometimes I would jog over from our mobile home to the mansion to visit with my mom. One afternoon I started jogging over to visit her and, of course, I looked just adorable — like most people when they are at home and not expecting anyone to see them. My hair was up in curlers and I had on my jogging suit and my "tenny pumps." As I left my yard and got out by the fence, I heard voices and looked up. There were some people taking my picture. Luckily, I didn't see how the pictures came out. I'm not sure I wanted to.

Another time, I just had washed my hair and put it up in rollers and was all comfortable to have dinner and spend a quiet evening at home with my little family. But most husbands aren't programmed to know exactly when their wives want to go out and when they don't and mine is no different. He picked that time to want me to go to the store to get something for him.

Let me set the scene. There always were people at the gate. Bless their hearts, that was all right, but I did want them to see me looking a little better or at least halfway presentable. But, being a dutiful wife, I got into my car and went down the hill and through the gate. I thought I was doing fine because there didn't seem to be too many people there.

But a friend of mine was in the parking lot across the street and she motioned for me to come over. I didn't want to offend her, so I drove across the street. It wasn't long before my car was surrounded by people wanting my autograph. My friend got a pen and started signing my name and hers. It really was funny in a way.

Priscilla once found herself being scolded by a stranger in the grocery store. "Priscilla wasn't wearing an outfit that the woman thought was right for Elvis Presley's wife," Susie remembers. "So the lady goes up to her and gets in her face and says, 'What do you mean coming out in public dressed like that? You're married to Elvis Presley.' "

Once someone knew you were Elvis' relative, there was one request you heard again and again — "Bring me something from Graceland." The more you heard it, the harder it was to come up with something original to bring back. Edie once thought of what she felt was a really original souvenir. "I had Elvis sign a roll of toilet tissue from Graceland and brought it back to a bunch of the girls at college," she laughs. The girls were just as glad to get that as they would have been to get an entire piece of furniture from some other house. That's just the kind of appeal that Elvis had.

Of course, the fans didn't make that a one-way street. They sent things to Graceland as well. When Donna worked there, it was her job to open the fan mail and see that it was answered. It was a pretty exciting job, she says.

"I enjoyed hearing from all over the world. Some of the letters we'd get, I couldn't read because they were in a different language. I just wrote a letter back in English," she explains. "I didn't send a form letter. I handwrote every letter. I felt like anybody who took the time and effort to write to Graceland should have a personal letter in return — even if they couldn't read it. I would just write back and say how good it was to hear from them and tell them something about Elvis and what was going on at Graceland."

Letters weren't the only thing that Donna found in the envelopes addressed to Graceland. "Probably the funniest thing we ever got was a pair of ladies' underwear. It was obvious they had been worn. I just laughed, but after that, I did start opening the mail with a letter opener," she says.

Just as Donna knew it was her job to see to it that every letter writer got a personal answer, the family all knew that they were responsible for not disgracing the Presley name. When your name and your behavior stands for a whole family, "you have to be 'on' all the time," Susie says. "You have to present a pleasant face."

"We've always had to carry his name," Donna says. "Anything we said or anything we did, we had to be very careful.

You look at Elvis, he didn't just walk around in old blue jeans and tennis shoes and a sweatshirt, you know.

"People look at us and they say, 'That's Elvis' cousin, you know.' They wonder what we're doing or why we're dressed the way we are. After Elvis' death, they would ask, 'If Elvis liked you so much, how come he didn't leave you any money?' I always just say, 'Why didn't Elvis leave YOU any money?' That money was Elvis'. He made it and he left it to his daughter. She deserved it."

The fans, Donna says, just transferred their love of Elvis to his family. "They would just come up and start talking to me, like they had known me forever. They felt that close to Elvis."

Finding people hiding outside your house or outside Graceland wasn't all that unusual when you were related to Elvis. Once when Donna was leaving her mother's house to go home, she spotted a man lying out in the grass by the mail box. Donna went back inside to tell her dad about the man being out there. Earl and one of his friends went outside to see what the man wanted, but when he spotted them, he jumped up and ran. When they caught up with him, he said he had lost his sunglasses and was looking for them.

"When my dad and Bill went back over to where the man had been lying down, they found a copperhead snake," Donna remembers. "The whole time, that man didn't know what he was next to out there. Can you imagine?"

Nash decided if there was one snake, there might be more. She didn't want to get to know any snakes on a personal basis and she felt other people might not want to either, so after that she made a point of warning those who were struck with Elvis fever that they might be struck by something else. As she explained:

> There was a lady who used to lie out there in the grass and read. One morning, as I started to go somewhere, I stopped and told her she shouldn't be lying there because snakes might be crawling around. I think she took my advice because I didn't see her out there anymore.

Another time, Nash had to help out a woman who kept telling her that she had gotten lost on Graceland property:

> One evening when we were having dinner, a lady drove up into our yard. I went out and asked her how she had gotten there. She said she just drove in. She thought she could get through to the street behind us, she said. I had my doubts about that because you don't drive through a private gate onto private property to get to a public street. But I said, "Lady, you've taken a wrong turn." After she had gotten in there, though, she couldn't get out. I had to turn her car around for her. And she left. I must admit, though, she was a nice lady. Over the years, we met a lot of people who were sweet and courteous, even if they did tell us they took a wrong turn or gave some other excuse for showing up in our front yard.

With people always watching you, wanting all sorts of souvenirs from Graceland and asking for their milk cartons to be touched, it was easy to become cynical quickly.

"There was an insecurity," Donna says. "When I was a teenager, Elvis was the ultimate. People would come up to me and they would be friendly and I would think, 'Why are you being so nice to me? Are you being nice because I'm Elvis' cousin? Because you want to get close to me in order to get close to Elvis?' That antenna always was going up.

"It was an automatic defense. We all still have this sort of wall that we only let certain people around. It's for self-preservation. It's saying to those people, 'I'm not going to let you hurt me. I'm not going to let you get through to my family or to get to my family through me.' "

If the Presley cousins have acquired a healthy suspicion of people's motives, it's probably because they've been taught it since the cradle. "You learn from an early age how to gauge people when you are related to someone rich or famous. Elvis was both," Donna says. There always was one Presley or another watching out to be sure Donna and her cousins weren't being taken advantage of.

"One night Susie was with Terry Blackwood and I was with Cecil," Edie remembers. "We were out in back of Graceland. Elvis was having a party and there was so much commotion. You could hear that they were having a blast. And Uncle Vester came up and said, 'Well, are y'all okay?' He was checking, making sure the guys were there with us and not hanging out to get to Elvis. Because people really would do that."

Taking your friends to your house is a common thing, especially when you are young. You and your buddies visit back and forth at each other's homes. Each of you has different neat games and toys and it's fun to be in somebody else's element for a while. It was the same with Donna and the other Presley cousins. Visiting friends' homes was fun. And they certainly always wanted to visit you back. After all, Graceland was the ultimate playground. There was a swimming pool and all the other "toys" Elvis provided for his family. And then there was Elvis. Bringing friends to Graceland was more common than most people might imagine.

"If we wanted to bring friends over, all we had to do was just take them up there," Donna says. "The real question was whether we felt the person wanted to be up there to be with us or if they just wanted to get a chance to see Elvis.

"Usually the ones we did take up there were the ones who didn't ask to go rather than the ones who did ask.

"Whenever we did take friends up to Graceland, Elvis always treated them graciously and made them feel welcome. Of course, they always left with more admiration and respect for Elvis than when they went in."

Another problem was the lack of privacy. "When I was working at Graceland, we lived just around the corner on Winchester," Donna remembers. "I had to change my phone number at least every three months because people would get my phone number and they would call — I mean, it's not that I minded them calling to talk about Elvis — but they would call at 3 and 4 o'clock in the morning.

"I had two small kids and I had to get up and go to

work. I had a life, too. I'd have people coming to my door in the middle of the night, knocking on my door. All because I was a family member, just a cousin."

Elvis' family also has learned that you don't share everything you know with everybody. Donna says, "Uncle Vernon used to say, 'What you hear on this hill, stays on this hill' and he was right about that. You can't understand what it's like to see all these 'Elvis was an alien' stories on the front of tabloids. Even if no one believed those stories, it would hurt to see them when they were about somebody you loved. Then to think that some people do believe them, that's really bad.

"It's even worse when the source of the stories is some member of the family or someone who was supposed to have been Elvis' friend, because in addition to seeing the story, there's the betrayal."

You didn't even have to be directly related to the singer to find yourself in the middle of the phenomenon that was Elvis Presley. After Buddy married Donna, he began to understand what she had lived with all her life.

"I came to realize that Elvis' family was just like every other family. They laughed and cried, they argued and played together. They loved each other," he says. "It wasn't his family that was different, it was other people's concept of his family. When I married Donna, I saw how people's reaction to you and their feelings toward you began to change.

"I began to notice that my friends' attitude toward me changed. It wasn't, 'Hey, Buddy, let's go fishing' anymore. They seemed to be wondering what I could do for them now that I was a member of the Presley family."

Just as being related to Elvis created some problems, it also led to the solutions to some of them. "I wouldn't have had to deal with the things I've dealt with if I hadn't been related to Elvis," Susie says. "But, on the other hand, I wouldn't have learned how to deal with people and how to deal with my own insecurities. Since Elvis was older than we were, we were able to watch what he was going through and sort of sidetrack a lot of those things because we saw what it was doing to him. With his being in the limelight and being who he was, I think it gave us a sense that we could do whatever we wanted to do because he was a perfect example of that.

"When he first started, he had no money and no support in the music industry. What happened to him was the American Dream. We grew up learning to think, 'I can do it.' I don't think we would have learned that lesson as well if we hadn't been related to Elvis."

For Edie, who has chosen a profession that puts her in the public eye, Elvis' lessons of "You can do it!" still support her when she starts a new project or gets an idea about one she might like to try. "When I was at Graceland, I would talk about ideas I had for holding some seminar or another and Elvis would give me ideas. A lot of the things we talked about, I've accomplished," she says.

"There were a lot of good times at Graceland," Donna says. "It's hard for people to understand, I know, but mostly we just thought of Elvis as our cousin and Graceland as home. We didn't see Elvis the entertainer, we saw Elvis the man."

As Nash said, "Regardless of all the unusual things that happened there, we all loved living on the hill called Graceland."

"Sometimes I get lonely in a room full of people."

BEING ELVIS PRESLEY HAD its ups and downs. The money meant Elvis could do anything he wanted to do, buy anything he wanted to buy. The fame meant he had given up his privacy and his ability to take anyone at face value. It made him a complex man, fun-loving and childlike, lonely and brooding.

One of the manifestations of his little boy side was the pets he kept at Graceland. At various times, there were dogs, birds, horses and even a monkey. Just as he did with many things in his life, Elvis started simply with the pets and then kept adding on until the whole thing was completely out of hand.

There were the peacocks. Their appeal was obvious. They are beautiful birds. They also are noisy birds, a trait that probably didn't endear Elvis to his neighbors. The peacocks always were getting out and Earl and his co-workers would have to go through the neighborhood rounding them up. It was the birds' strange eating habits, however, that finally made them unwelcome at Graceland. "He had peacocks on the grounds until they started pecking the paint off his Stutz," Susie says. "Then they became the property of the local zoo."

Practically every kid in the South grows up with at least

one pet dog. Elvis just grew up with his a little later than most. Getlow was Elvis' chow. Getlow had the impression that he, not Elvis, was the owner of Graceland. Chows are notoriously hardheaded and stubborn and Getlow had honed that trait to perfection. Talking to the walls at Graceland got you about as much response as talking to Getlow.

Put Getlow up against Susie, who isn't noted in her family for giving in easily, and you've got a real battle of wills. Which is exactly what happened one day when Getlow got out of the fence at Graceland. Nash told the story of the day Susie and Getlow squared off:

> *When Getlow got out, he went through the woods to the street behind Graceland. Now, you would have to know Susie to appreciate this scene, because patience is not one of her virtues. Getlow decided he liked it out in the woods and he didn't want to come back home. She pleaded with him and he sat there looking at her as if to say, "You've got to be kidding." Well, to make a long story short, she picked him up and carried, wagged and pulled him along saying, "I don't care whose dog you are, you are going home."*

Getlow, unfortunately, had his share of medical problems. More than once, Delta and Nash had to take him to the vet. As Nash pointed out, sometimes Getlow didn't remember he was a dog:

> *One day Delta and I started to take him to the vet. Well, no one told him that he was a dog and that he should ride in the back seat and Aunt Nash should ride in the front seat with Aunt Delta. Getlow climbed in the front seat and I had to sit in the back. I think he won the argument without a contest.*

During another of Getlow's illnesses, Elvis flew the dog, accompanied by Linda Thompson and one of Linda's girlfriends, to Boston to see a veterinarian. The clinic there specialized in the disease from which Getlow suffered. Elvis' dog was going to have the best chance possible to recover. But even the best medical care money could buy couldn't save Getlow. When the dog died, Elvis cried. And for months after that, every time he thought about Getlow, he started crying again. Nash said:

> The dog was flown to Boston to see a certain veterinarian there, so I guess he had to be a pretty special dog for his owner to take such good care of him. I guess that's why he didn't think he should have to ride in the back seat.

Elvis also bought a Pomeranian. Somehow, the dog got the name Edmond. Edmond apparently didn't understand about how the person who had bought him was Elvis Presley and how he was supposed to be Elvis' dog. Edmond immediately bonded with Delta. Nash explained:

> Elvis used to call down and have someone bring Edmond up to his bedroom. He would run across Elvis' bed, turn around and come right back downstairs to Delta. Elvis said to her one time, "Aunt Delta, I used to have a dog."

Finally accepting the fact that even Elvis wasn't going to be able to boss Edmond around, Elvis gave the dog to Delta. Edmond lived at Graceland with Delta until he died in 1986.

There also were two sheepdogs at Graceland. They, like Getlow, found great joy in escaping from the fence and romping through the woods. Nash and her family spent a great deal of time chasing them and bringing them back to Graceland. Elvis didn't seem to mind if his pets were a little stubborn and a lot adventuresome. It just seemed to be a reflection of the child in their owner.

Scatter, the monkey, was another pet who seemed to have more than a touch of the bad boy in him. And, as Nash explained, he was another who was spoiled terribly by his owner:

> One time, Scatter got loose in the kitchen. No one in the kitchen saw the humor in his being loose, especially Earl. Someone told Earl to catch Scatter and hold him. Being a brave soul, my husband said, "No way!" and ran out in the back yard. After that, Scatter had to spend his time in his own house. But it was the beginning of the good life for him, because they built him a house with air conditioning and heat.

As if all the animals running around didn't create enough of a circus, there was Elvis' other love — practical jokes. The more elaborate they were, the better he liked them. Because he had the money, Elvis could indulge himself in expensive jokes that other people might have loved to pull, but couldn't afford.

Take the room at Graceland that's come to be known as the Jungle Room. The furniture in there is massive, trimmed in wood and covered with a fuzzy, fake fur fabric. It's not your typical down-South type sofa and chair. Why did Elvis choose that to anchor his decorating scheme for this room? Because of something Vernon had said.

The day before Elvis bought the furniture for the Jungle Room, Vernon and his fiancee, Sandy, had been in a furniture store in Whitehaven. Vernon had seen some furniture he really didn't like and wondered out loud to Sandy who would buy furniture that ugly.

The next morning, he found out. When he got to Graceland, the delivery truck was outside and the men were removing one of the windows from the den so that they could get the furniture inside. It was too big to go in any other way.

Vernon called Sandy and said, "Now I know who would buy that furniture." Then he called Elvis on the intercom. "There are a bunch of guys down here trying to decide where to put this furniture. You want to come down and tell them where you want it?" Nash, sitting in the kitchen, said you could hear Elvis' laugh all over Graceland.

Though Elvis bought the furniture there as a joke, the "Jungle Room" became one of Elvis' favorite places, family members say, because Lisa Marie liked it when she was a small child. She found that the oversized chair was a perfect place for her to curl up for a nap. The chair that cradled his child always held a special place in the singer's heart even if it didn't get him any cover stories in home decorating magazines.

Elvis always was pulling practical jokes on the guys. One day, they decided to get even with him. At the time, Elvis had a Mynah bird. It had gotten an education in language not only from people who worked to help it learn phrases, but from overhearing what people said a lot. While Elvis was teaching it to whistle at girls and say such things as "Get out and go to the Devil!" the guys were teaching it some other phrases.

One night, Elvis and the guys came into Graceland late and the house was dark. Elvis, standing with his back to the bird, turned on the light and heard, "Turn out the light!" "Put up your hands!" Elvis was convinced that Graceland was being robbed. His immediate reaction was to raise his hands and tell the intruder to take anything he wanted, but not to hurt anyone. After he stood there with his hands in the air for a few moments, the voice repeated a phrase heard often at Graceland — "S-h-h, you'll wake up Elvis!" Elvis realized then that he was being held hostage by his own Mynah bird. He dropped to the floor with relief and laughter.

"I thought he would come unglued. He absolutely was rolling in the floor," Donna recalls. "It was really something to see."

Someone finally had pulled a trick on Elvis equal to the ones he pulled on them.

Elvis' fans — and he loved his fans — also caused more than a small amount of commotion at Graceland. The gates at Elvis' home were well-guarded. But his fans were imaginative. They always were coming up with new ways to get past that last barrier between them and the person they wanted to visit. There were several incidents that Nash remembered:

I guess one of the funniest and most unusual things that happened was when the two girls from Mississippi State had themselves crated up, put into a truck and brought to Graceland marked "Russian Wolfhounds." They thought Elvis would have to accept and sign for them. When they arrived at Graceland, they didn't get past Vester at the gate.

One night Elvis was having a party at the mansion for family and friends. The guard came in with a really pretty girl. Elvis looked at her and said, "Hi, party crasher, where did you come from?" She said, "I just climbed over the fence and jumped down — into the mud no less." Elvis told the maid to clean up her shoes and then told the guard to take her down to the gate. Before she left, she made a phone call to somebody and said, "I bet you can't guess where I am." I suppose the other person couldn't guess because she said, "In the kitchen at Graceland." I guess she accomplished what she wanted to and Elvis only laughed about it.

One day, two ladies drove up to the front gate and hit the gate with their car. Vester went out there to investigate and the ladies said the Lord had sent them there to talk to Elvis. To that, Vester said, "Ladies, if the Lord had sent you, the gates would have opened."

One lady got past the guard one day and drove up to the front door of Graceland and said she was married to Elvis. It was her house and she was going in whether anyone wanted her to or not, because Elvis was expecting her. Now this was several years after Elvis passed away. She wouldn't leave, so the guard had to call the police to get her out of the driveway.

Several people have jumped into the swimming pool at Graceland. A lady got in one night, jumped in the pool and wouldn't get out. The guard had to jump in and bring her out.

Then there was the Alabama woman who, for some reason, thought she was going to marry Elvis. The lady, a widow with four children, even had her parents convinced she was marrying Elvis. Her mother had an engagement announcement published in their weekly newspaper. The announcement said that the woman and "E.A. Presley, son of Mr. Vernon Presley and the late Mrs. Gladys Smith Presley, will be married April 17, 1976, before their families and close friends."

After the announcement appeared, the woman's family was swamped with calls from journalists from all over the world. She insisted that she had met Elvis earlier in a Memphis hospital and that their love was something sacred to both of them. Her children, she said, were thrilled at the prospect of having Elvis become their stepfather.

The town of Athens, Alabama, was invaded and overrun by reporters, cameramen and Elvis fans on the announced wedding day. The bride showed, but the much-anticipated groom, who had insisted from the first that there was to be no wedding, didn't.

Whether they were climbing over his fence, planning to marry him or attending his concerts, Elvis always put his fans first. "He always made sure they got their money's worth," Donna says. "He would tell you right quick, 'They're depending on me to give them entertainment and to give them a show and that's what I'm going to do.' "

He didn't just look at his fans as fans, she explains. "They were friends and they were family and they felt that. That's what put Elvis on the top and that's why he's still there today."

As generously as Elvis gave to his fans, he gave to charities and to people in need.

"He was such a generous person. He cared so much about

people and gave so much to everyone," Donna says. "He
bought houses for people, cars for people, clothes and jewelry for them, paid their bills. It's just amazing how much
money he spent on other people. He just wanted them to be
happy.

"He tried to make life easier for them. He tried to give
them things that he didn't have when he was a little boy,
things they couldn't afford. They say it's better to give than
to receive. I think Elvis carried that one to the limit and beyond. To him, it was much better to give than to receive.

"He loved to hear people say, 'I never thought I could
have this' or 'I never dreamed that I could go to this place'
or 'I never thought in a million years I'd have a home like
this or a new automobile or clothes or jewelry like this.'

"But, then, that was Elvis. Everything to the limit. If he
bought himself something, he made sure everybody else had
one, too. He didn't just get his wealth and keep it to himself,
he gave to everybody whether he knew the person or not."

Over the years, Elvis donated millions of dollars to charities. Early in his career, Elvis had done a benefit concert for
Memphis charities. The concert had raised $50,000. Even
though he wasn't able to schedule another charity concert,
he sent a $50,000 check each year. The two Memphis news-
papers held an annual fund drive for local charities around
Christmas. Every year, Vernon and Elvis went to the newspaper office with a $1,000 check for each charity. He do-
nated money to hospitals and to schools. More than that, he
often visited the hospitals and schools to talk to the children, to encourage them and to give them hope. In a world
where time was money, Elvis was generous with both.

Once a policeman who was one of Elvis' friends told the
singer about a Memphis child dying of cancer who had said
he wanted a letter from Elvis before he died. What he got
was several visits from Elvis. Even after the family moved to
Florida, Elvis continued to write to the child and to send
him gifts.

Often when Elvis was shopping for new cars, he would
go up to a young couple or an older woman in the show-

room and ask, "What color do you like?" They would tell him, thinking they were engaged in simple showroom conversation with another customer. They were, instead, putting in their order for a car paid for by Elvis.

When "Teddy Bear" was an Elvis hit, the singer sent a truckload of his teddy bears to the National Foundation for Infantile Paralysis to be auctioned off.

In January, 1964, he purchased the late President Roosevelt's yacht, The Potomac, with the intention of donating it to the March of Dimes. By February, however, the March of Dimes had consulted its attorneys and determined that the group could not accept the gift. Elvis gave it instead to St. Jude's Hospital. The hospital then used the yacht as a fund-raising tool.

Late that same year, Elvis heard about a woman who needed a new wheelchair. He bought it and delivered it — and $200 — personally.

The Motion Pictures Relief Fund was conducting a big fund–raising drive in 1965. Elvis gave the group $50,000 outright and pledged 2 percent of his income from one of his movies as well. His total contribution to the group that helps actors and actresses who are "down on their luck" as well as retired actors and actresses, was $240,000.

Elvis literally brought the fund-raising effort home in 1968 when he held the first public auction of his personal possessions. The city of Memphis was packed with people eager to bid on something that Elvis had used or had touched. The auction raised more than $100,000 and all of it went to charity.

In 1970, Elvis gave the Los Angeles Police Department's Community Relations Fund $7,000. The money was used to buy toys for needy children, uniforms for the LAPD Marching Band and special jackets for explosives-sniffing dogs.

Three years later, when a Boy Scout camp in Louisiana lost its equipment to vandals, Elvis gave the group $1,000. In 1975, he gave the Jerry Lewis Muscular Dystrophy Telethon $5,000.

When his Aunt Nash became a minister of the Assembly

of God Church, Elvis paid $20,000 for some land in Walls, Mississippi. The land, he told her, was for her church. The church put a building there and Nash's ministry in the Mississippi district began. When she started out, she said, the church didn't have a piano:

> When I first began pastoring the church at Walls, Mississippi, Elvis asked me if I had a piano for the church and I said, "No." So he asked me if I would like to have the one in the music room and, without hesitation, I said, "Yes, I would." He was referring to the Grand piano that Priscilla had gotten for him. Years before this, Elvis and Priscilla were watching a show on which a popular pianist was playing a gold Grand piano. Elvis liked it so much that Priscilla decided to get one for him.

Priscilla chose a nine-foot Grand and had it gold-leafed, then delivered to Graceland. Now the piano would be moving on, everyone thought, to Nash's church. The problem was that the piano wouldn't fit into the church building. Nash continued:

> I finally went to a music shop in Memphis and asked one of the men about trading the Grand piano for one that our building would accommodate. The man said he would trade and I picked a pine Wurlitzer. I took a picture of it home with me and went over and showed it to Elvis. I asked him if he would mind my trading for it. He said, "Aunt Nash, you do what you need to do because I gave the piano to you."

(Years later, Nash tried to track down what had happened to the Grand piano after she traded it in. Actually, it was bought by a private citizen in Memphis and donated for display to Graceland for a number of years. It now is on display in the Country Music Hall of Fame in Nashville.)
Elvis didn't mind if you traded one of his gifts for some-

thing else. He didn't want you to trade it for something that was going to cost you more money, however. Earl learned that when he decided to trade a car that Elvis had bought for him.

Earl didn't like the new car as well as he liked another brand of car he had had before. So once when Elvis was out of town, Earl traded the one Elvis had given him for one made by the other company. The car for which he traded cost more than the one Elvis had bought, so Earl financed the difference.

"When Elvis got back," Earl says, "he asked how I was liking the car. I said, 'Me and the bank like it fine.' He asked me what I meant and I told him what I had done. Elvis gave me the money for the difference in the two prices right then. He said, 'I didn't buy you a car for you to go into debt.' "

John T. Crosby was another beneficiary of Elvis' generosity. Crosby, who now is public relations director for a realty company in Alabama, once had aspirations of being a professional musician. More than 30 years ago, Crosby was with a group called The Gentrys.

"We performed on the Ted Mack Amateur Hour at the Tennessee State Fair and won," he explains. "All of our equipment was used. Elvis had been there and heard us.

"Later, we were told to go to a certain music store in Memphis and pick out some new equipment. When we selected our equipment and looked at the sales slip, written on the bottom was 'TCB.' That was the way Elvis did things — anonymously.

"It didn't have to be for people in Memphis either. When he was on the road, even at the start when he didn't have much, he would help people. He continued that throughout his life.

"What he did changed my life. I had had a rough childhood and his believing in me turned me around," Crosby said.

Elvis gave a special moment to another child, but this time it wasn't done anonymously. Once when he was doing a concert, he began tossing scarves to people in the audience. It was something he did all the time and an Elvis scarf was a prized possession to take away from one of his appearances. On this night, though, there was a little girl who kept trying to catch one of the scarves. It especially was difficult for her to get a scarf because she was blind. Every time she almost had one, it was snatched from her grip by a grown-up. Elvis stopped the concert and told the security guards to bring the little girl up on stage.

Many people saw what Elvis did and the story has been told many times — most of the times incorrectly. What everybody reads is that Elvis gave the little girl one of his necklaces. What he really gave her was one of his rings.

He slipped it off his finger and threaded a scarf through it. He tied a knot to hold the ring, then tied the scarf around the little girl's neck. "Now you hold on to that," he told her, "and when people ask you, you tell them Elvis gave it to you. Don't let anybody take that away from you."

Then he had the guards take her back to her seat and went on with the concert.

Sometimes, the material things that Elvis gave took a back seat to the gift of his notice and concern. At least that's what one little boy thought.

Buzz Richey, who now is a businessman living in Forrest City, Arkansas, was elementary-school age when he met Elvis. Buzz was on a plane bound for Dallas. Elvis also was on the plane. It caused quite a stir to have the singer on the flight. Everyone was going up to the first–class area and asking for his autograph. Everyone except the shy young boy who just remained in his seat and watched what was going on. Finally, Buzz asked a woman on the plane to get Elvis' autograph for him. Elvis found out about the little boy who was too shy to come up and ask for an autograph.

He told the flight attendants to get Buzz and bring him up to the front of the plane. Buzz was a little in awe when he first took his seat beside Elvis, but the singer quickly made him feel at ease. They talked about where Elvis had been and where Buzz had been. They discussed what they were going to do when they got home. Elvis autographed the jacket

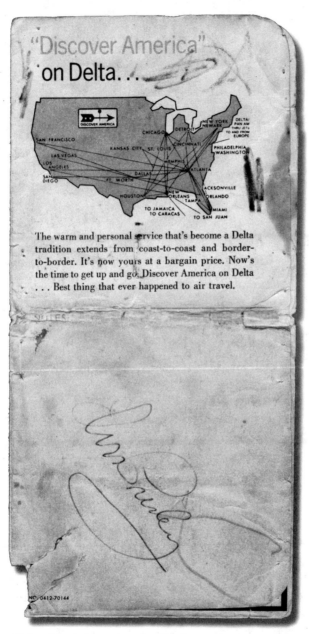

Airline ticket jacket autographed by Elvis Presley for Buzz Richey when he was a youngster.

that held Buzz's airline tickets. And Buzz spent the rest of the flight in first–class with Elvis Presley.

Elvis always had a soft spot in his heart for children and he was a little concerned about this young boy arriving in Dallas alone. When the plane landed, he told Buzz to stay in his seat and let everyone else get off.

"My parents were waiting for me and they were getting a little concerned when I didn't get right off the plane," Richey remembers. "Then their jaws dropped when they saw who I got off the plane with."

Elvis delivered Buzz safely to his waiting parents, stayed to chat a while and then was on his way. Little boys often misplace things — their lunch money, their homework, their treasured baseball cards. And Richey may have lost some of his childhood possessions along the way as he's grown older. But he still has his autographed ticket jacket from the flight he took with Elvis Presley.

As generous as Elvis was, as unselfishly as he gave to others, one would assume he would be beloved by everyone. That wasn't the case. In fact, Elvis' life was threatened a number of times. Nash recalled one of those:

> I think he feared for his life on many occasions. Elvis was appearing in Las Vegas once when the wife of one of Elvis' employees received a phone call from a man saying he was going to kill Elvis. The people in charge of the hotel where he was performing told him. He didn't have to go on, but he said he wanted to anyway.
>
> Every night during that appearance, he told my brother Vernon, Lisa and Priscilla goodbye.
>
> All the guys were poised and ready to attack should anyone make a suspicious move. They had a beeper on a doctor at the hospital just in case anything happened. They had an ambulance on standby if Elvis should need to be transferred to the hospital.
>
> One night, a man in the audience called out Elvis' name. Elvis fell to his knees (He said he didn't want

the man to get too good a shot at him.) and said,
"Yeah?" The man said, "You forgot to sing, 'Suspi-
cious Minds.' "

There definitely was a price to be paid for being Elvis
Presley. On his *How Great Thou Art* album, Elvis sang a
song called, "Where No One Stands Alone." In one of the
verses, there is the phrase "I may be a king in a palace so tall
with great riches to call my own, but I don't know a thing in
this whole wide world that's worse than being alone." There
was an irony to Elvis' singing that. He probably knew what
those words meant better than anyone else in the world.

"You know, I guess fame and fortune is something that
we've all dreamed about and thought, 'Oh, it would be so
wonderful to be rich and to be famous, to be able to do this
or to have that,' " Donna says. "But it has its price and it's a
great price to pay.

"Elvis couldn't go out like other people. He couldn't go
Christmas shopping with the hustle and bustle of the rest of
the crowd like we can. To me, that's a lot of the fun. The
crowds at Christmas are what makes it exciting. It's fun to
see all the Christmas decorations and the people and all.

"We can go to Opryland or Libertyland and ride the rides
and have a good time. If there's a movie we want to see, all
we have to do is hop in the car, go to the theater and watch
it.

"Because of Elvis' fame, he wasn't allowed to do that. If
he wanted to go Christmas shopping, he had to wait until
the malls closed and then have them open back up for him.
If he wanted to see a movie, he had to wait until everything
closed down and then open it back up so he could see the
movie with his family and friends. If he wanted to go to
Libertyland, he had to wait until it closed, then go in the
middle of the night to have a good time.

"No matter where he went, he always was recognized.
Everything he did was a news story. Fame isn't always all it's
cracked up to be. But I don't believe Elvis would have been
happy doing anything else. He was born to be a star."

Just as he couldn't "go out and play" freely, Elvis found he couldn't attend church, either. "When Mom started pastoring in 1974," Donna says, "she asked Elvis to come to the church, especially since he had bought the property for the church to go on. And he said, 'I'd love to come, Aunt Nash, but I don't want to be a distraction. Our minds should be on the sermon and not on Elvis Presley. I have too much respect for you and for my God to do that.' "

Elvis also bore the heavy burden of being a role model for others. It was not a position he sought, but one that seemed to find him anyway. Even though he didn't encourage others to be like him, some people found him an easy scapegoat when things didn't go well in their lives. As Nash said:

> This one man said he was such an avid Elvis fan that he wanted to be just like Elvis. In fact, he said he wanted to be Elvis. He said he dressed just like him. He wanted to sing like Elvis and he started taking drugs.
>
> I can't remember everything the man said in his interview, but the essence of it was that he wanted to be just like Elvis and that desire had put him on the road to total destruction. He said when he hit rock bottom, he gave his life over to the Lord. I say, "Thank God for that."
>
> But may I say, in all due respect to that young man and as a member of Elvis Presley's family, that I do not think Elvis would have approved of anyone taking up his bad habits or of anyone patterning his life after Elvis'. I know he would have appreciated this man's liking his music and wanting to sing like him, but I do believe he would have said to this young man, "Man, don't do it. It's not worth it."
>
> It's about time people took responsibility for their own faults and quit blaming Elvis for their mistakes and for everything bad that has happened to them.

Elvis' life was sort of a maze. Turn here and find fame and fortune. Turn there and the way's blocked because of the crowd. Turn here and meet new friends. Turn there and wonder if they really are your friends after all. He spent a great deal of time thinking about things like that. It frustrated him that he couldn't know exactly what other people were thinking about him.

"He said, 'I know I have all these fans, but does anybody really love me?' " Susie recalls. "Once he said, 'I wish I could be loved just for me.' "

He and Nash talked often about the problem. Edie recalls, "Nash would call me and say, 'Edie, you need to pray for Elvis, he's having a really rough time.' We prayed about that a lot."

"Elvis always had a lot of people around him," Donna says, "and it made for a lot of good times, but I know a lot of it was confining as well. He really never knew just exactly who really, truly loved him. Most of us know about our relationships with other people. We know if they truly love us. But Elvis always had a doubt in his mind. That's really got to be a very painful position to be in."

Sometimes, when she would see Elvis like that, she says, she would wish she were closer to his age. "Perhaps I could have been a confidante to him. Sometimes it helps just to have someone to listen to you and to know that regardless of what you are saying it doesn't matter to them, they care about you.

"There is a down side to fame. Elvis was very good at camouflaging things. You had to get to know him really well to know when he was conning you into thinking everything was okay when it wasn't. He never really achieved what he wanted for himself — to know for sure that he was loved just for himself. And he wanted peace of mind. That was something he never really found. Elvis let himself down more than he ever let anyone else down."

As Nash pointed out, "I've heard Elvis say many times, 'Aunt Nash, sometimes I get lonely in a room full of people.' "

12

"Please don't forget me."

JUST AS IT WASN'T always easy being Elvis Presley, it wasn't always easy being Mrs. Elvis Presley. Priscilla learned a little bit more about this every day. Elvis was on the road a lot with concerts. He was out of town a lot when he was making movies. Sometimes Priscilla traveled with him and sometimes she didn't.

When she was at home at Graceland, Lisa Marie provided a distraction for her. And she had friends to talk to and familiar places to go. When she and Elvis were out of town together, he went about his business and Priscilla was left alone to find new distractions in a town where she didn't have friends, family or places she knew.

Once again, she confided in Donna. "Priscilla and I were close," Donna says. "She would say, 'I don't think I can handle seeing Elvis kiss this woman in a movie.' She had her insecurities as any woman would being married to Elvis and having millions of women throw themselves at him. She got lonely. That was something that Elvis couldn't take. He thought she should understand that the travel was part of his career. It's not fair, because I'm sure there were other women in his life while she was married to Elvis."

Elvis' movies weren't the kind where the hero rides off into the sunset with his faithful horse. In Elvis' movies, the guy always got the girl — sometimes lots of girls. Naturally, there were plenty of pretty young starlets and beautiful established actresses around all the time. The natural outcome was rumors that flew constantly about Elvis and this co-star or that struggling actress. There were paternity suits. They were unsuccessful, but even if the courts said your husband wasn't some child's father, you still didn't like the fact that someone claimed he was.

Sometimes there was more truth than rumor to the stories. "There were a lot of women in Elvis' life. They came in different shapes and sizes. They were blond, brunette. The ones that I knew personally were just Southern girls. I truly believe he looked for something close to his roots," Donna says. "Aunt Delta used to say that he had one upstairs and one waiting for him downstairs all the time."

Elvis never would have tolerated the same behavior in Priscilla. But somehow it seems that Elvis didn't realize he was applying a double standard. He didn't love the other girls he was with. He loved Priscilla. As long as he didn't fall in love with someone else, he seemed to think he was being faithful to his wife.

Donna says she feels Elvis "truly loved Priscilla. I believe that Priscilla really loved Elvis and he loved her and Lisa Marie. But obstacles got in the way.

"Their marriage came to an end because of outside pressures. If they had been just Elvis and Priscilla Presley from Tupelo, Mississippi, they would not have divorced. I'm sure the stress and strain of knowing that millions of women were always trying to get close to Elvis and just spend any amount of time they could with him was hard on Priscilla," Donna says. "And Elvis had to be away a great deal. It was just too hard for her."

The same people who were keeping Elvis from his family were keeping him from his wife as well. And Elvis was putting up some of the barriers, too. It seemed to Priscilla that ever since she had become a mother, Elvis no longer regarded her as someone who should be thought of in a sexual sense. Mothers were to be put on a pedestal, sort of worshiped from afar. They were too special to involve in everyday things such as sex.

The problem was many-fold. Elvis and Priscilla weren't communicating physically. And they weren't communicating verbally. Sometimes they argued, but it wasn't the things they said that were the problem. It was the things that were left unsaid.

Priscilla didn't know how to deal with that lack of communication.

Elvis, meantime, was going from concert to concert, from movie to movie, from girl to girl. And he was going from hobby to hobby. "Nothing ever interested him for very long," Donna explains. One of the things that did catch his attention for a while was karate. He started taking lessons, learning all about it.

And he followed his usual pattern. If he was enjoying it, he wanted everybody else to be enjoying it, too. Soon Priscilla also was taking karate lessons. Her teacher was a man named Mike Stone.

After Elvis' interest in karate waned, Priscilla kept on with her lessons. And she began having an affair with Stone.

"I don't think it's fair to blame Priscilla until you've walked in her shoes," Donna says. "However, I do feel that the affair with Mike Stone did hurt Elvis immensely."

It took a lot to make Elvis angry enough to have one of those well-known bursts of temper, his family says. Finding out about Priscilla's affair was one of those things that pushed him over the edge. Nash said:

> *I know Elvis was condemned for the way he reacted toward the person he felt broke up his home. We've all read that Elvis threatened to kill this person. Maybe he did say something like that, but we all say things like that when we are hurt. It doesn't mean we are going to carry through with them.*
> *Elvis did tell me that he heard this man was going*

to try to keep him from his little girl. We can under-
stand and be moved with compassion and sympathy
for anyone going through an experience like that.

In early 1972, Priscilla told Elvis she was leaving. She came to get the things that belonged to her and Lisa Marie. "I know it was hard for Priscilla because she loved him a great deal at one time," Donna says.

When Priscilla arrived at Graceland to get her things, she went to Minnie's room. As usual, she found most of the women of the family there. She talked to them, told them she was leaving and cried as she kept begging, "Please don't forget me." That wasn't something that was likely to happen. The Presley family had taken Priscilla into their fold. She was a Presley. No matter what happened between her and Elvis, they would be concerned about her happiness.

"Of course, the family was very upset over Elvis and Priscilla's divorce," Donna says. "For one thing, it meant that Lisa Marie wouldn't be there all the time."

In August, 1972, Elvis filed for divorce from Priscilla. He listed as the reason "irreconcilable differences." Priscilla didn't contest the divorce. The divorce became final in October, 1973. Elvis and Priscilla were awarded joint custody of Lisa Marie. As the former Mr. and Mrs. Presley left the Santa Monica, California, courthouse, they didn't look like a couple who just had ended their marriage. Their arms around each other, their heads close together in conversation, they easily could have been mistaken for a couple who had just gotten a marriage license.

It was a continuation of what must, to some, have seemed like a long, strange relationship between Elvis and Priscilla. She had come to live at his house when she was a mere child. She stood by faithfully as his career soared. She ignored the stories that said he was going to marry each new co-star that came along. She married him and had his child. Now they were splitting up. But they still seemed to be friends. In fact, they probably were still friends even on the day they divorced.

They hadn't so much stopped loving one another as they

had simply found themselves at different places in their lives. Priscilla needed to be out, to have a life of her own. She always had been someone's daughter, someone's girlfriend, someone's wife or someone's mother. Now it was time for her to be Priscilla. She had to find out who she was, separate from anyone else. She had to know what she could do. Being married to Elvis meant she couldn't do that. Like two gears that once had fit together perfectly, their lives had worn over the years. Now they were out of sync and doing no one any good.

One thing they did remain in sync about was Lisa Marie. Both of her parents loved her, doted on her. Each only wanted what was best for her. Neither wanted to deny her the benefit of the other parent. Even if they couldn't be together, they both always would be there for their daughter.

Priscilla and Elvis walked to the end of the sidewalk, got into their separate cars and rode away. They both were starting new phases in their lives — Priscilla with a search for herself and for a career, Elvis with the same, all-consuming career but without a support he had thought he always could count on.

In 1972, Elvis had met Linda Thompson. Linda was the reigning Miss Tennessee when her path crossed Elvis'. She was beautiful, the kind of girl that any red-blooded American boy was bound to notice. She certainly wasn't about to escape the attention of Elvis that night when she attended one of the private movie screenings he often held at the Memphian Theater. One of Elvis' staff members had invited her, asking her if she would like to meet Elvis. She accepted and found herself the object of the singer's interest.

It wasn't long before Linda moved into Graceland and became the new woman in Elvis' life. Linda was showered with gifts of jewelry and furs. It was something Elvis did for people he cared about. He pampered her and indulged her. She did the same for him. Elvis' family liked Linda. They found her to be a down-to-earth person who seemed sincerely to care for Elvis. And she got along well with Lisa Marie.

"I liked Linda," Edie says. "She was a Southern girl, she knew what family meant, she didn't look down her nose at any of us. She even used to visit Nash's church."

Elvis' family thought she might become the singer's second wife. And, as Elvis told Nash, he thought about that, too:

> We talked about the kind of girl he wanted, if and when he decided to remarry. At the time, he was with Linda and he said, "Aunt Nash, right now Linda seems to be the type I would want. She's a Southern girl. She's kind and considerate, she doesn't use bad language and, most important, she has a deep love for God."

Elvis might have learned some things from his marriage to and divorce from Priscilla, but one thing he didn't learn was that in order to have a lasting relationship with a woman who truly loved him, he was going to have to make some changes in his lifestyle. Many of the things that drove away Priscilla — the isolation, the misuse of drugs and the rumored liaisons with other women — also wore on Linda. Their relationship lasted for the better part of five years, but it had begun to unravel long before then.

Linda found she had something else in common with Priscilla. She really cared for Elvis, she just didn't know how to help him.

"I think Linda truly loved Elvis and Elvis probably truly loved her. She was a good Southern lady for him," Edie says. "Of course, Priscilla probably was his real love. The lifestyle cost him Priscilla and eventually it cost him Linda."

When Linda no longer could cope with the lifestyle at Graceland, she, too, moved out. But, as he had with Priscilla, Elvis remained close to Linda. Once again, he and a woman he cared deeply about found they made much better friends than lovers.

In late 1976, Elvis met Ginger Alden. Even before they met, they had a mutual acquaintance. Ginger's father, a career Army man, had been present at Elvis' swearing in so many years before. Like most of Elvis' women, Ginger had long hair and soft eyes. They seemed to get along well and, by the beginning of 1977, Ginger was a part of the Graceland landscape. Elvis bought her a ring. Ginger insisted it was an engagement ring and that Elvis had proposed marriage to her. Insiders — both family and friends — had their doubts.

Donna's husband Buddy says one of Elvis' staff members told him that Elvis had made it plain he wasn't going to marry Ginger. "Once Elvis had told the guys this joke about a monkey who knew sign language. The joke ends with the monkey making one sign that this guy can't understand. So the guy says to the monkey's trainer, 'What does that mean?' And the trainer says, 'It means this monkey ain't gonna do that.'

"This person told me about one night when Elvis and the guys were sitting around Graceland and Ginger comes down from upstairs. She's showing off her ring to everybody and telling them that she and Elvis are going the next day to shop for wedding rings and a wedding dress.

"Then she turns around to talk to somebody else and her back is to Elvis. The guy said while she wasn't looking, Elvis made that sign for 'This monkey ain't gonna do that.' He said that's how they all knew that Elvis wasn't going to marry Ginger."

Buddy said that the man told him that by the middle of 1977, Ginger "knew she was on her way out at Graceland. She knew she was just one in a line of women."

What is certain is that Ginger knew neither she — nor any other future wife — was mentioned in Elvis' will.

Elvis had had a will drawn up early on in his career. "In that will," Donna explains, "everybody got something.

"Mom told us that Uncle Vernon said he had talked to Elvis and asked him to change his will because he (Vernon) felt that Elvis was overly influenced by certain members of the Memphis Mafia."

In 1977, Elvis asked his attorney to create a new will for him. In that one, signed by Elvis on March 3, 1977, Elvis makes definite arrangements for the care of his daughter,

Lisa Marie, "and any other lawful issue I might have," for his father and for his grandmother Minnie Mae Presley. Vernon was to serve as the executor of Elvis' will, in which the singer also provided for "such other relatives of mine living at the time of my death who, in the absolute discretion of my Trustee, are in need of emergency assistance for their health, education, support, comfortable maintenance and welfare."

After the deaths of both Vernon and Minnie, the will stated, Elvis' "lawful" children were to receive all the benefits of his estate.

Under Item IX, a "Spendthrift Provision," Elvis sought to protect Lisa Marie from the people he had feared the most in his lifetime — those who would pretend to care about her for an opportunity to share in the wealth of Elvis Presley. The will says that any bequests "contained herein for any female shall be for her sole and separate use, free from the debts, contracts and control of any husband she may ever have."

The will, which spelled out clearly who would benefit in the event of Elvis' death and how assets were to be handled as long as his children were minors, was witnessed by Ginger Alden, Charles F. Hodge and Ann Dewey Smith. No one knew it then, but in a little over five months, the will Elvis signed that day would go into effect.

Perhaps the timing of the new will showed that Elvis had something of a premonition about his death or maybe it was just that Elvis wanted to do what Vernon had asked him to do. And it did make provisions for any other children Elvis might have should he remarry.

Elvis apparently still entertained the idea of getting back together with Priscilla. Again, Buddy says he heard this from one of Elvis' staff members. "Elvis flew out to California to go to a PTA meeting for Lisa Marie in Los Angeles," Buddy explains. "The man said when Elvis got back on the plane, he said, 'Guess what, my old lady wants to have another kid and she wants me to be the daddy.' He said Elvis didn't really seem opposed to that idea at all."

Perhaps, his family believes, Elvis had come to accept the new Priscilla — the one who was independent, not an extension of him. "I think he encouraged Priscilla to do what she wanted to do. He felt that everyone has that right," Donna says. "He gave her space. He and Priscilla had talked about getting back together."

It might have happened, if Elvis had lived longer. Both he and Priscilla seemed to be at a place in their lives where they might have rebuilt a relationship. "Husbands and wives make mistakes," Nash said. "God can put those hearts back together again."

A reconciliation genuinely seems to have been in the offing. Priscilla openly admitted that she never had stopped loving Elvis.

Even though the remarriage never took place, Donna and the rest of the family still have a special spot in their hearts for Priscilla and Lisa Marie. "They've always been part of our family and they always will be," Donna says. "Occasionally I will write Priscilla a note and ask her how she's doing, just to let her know I'm thinking about her and Lisa Marie. I just wish them the best. You keep in touch. You don't have to be with a person on a day-to-day basis to care about them." As Nash explained:

Priscilla told me that Elvis had given her hope that they would get back together. Perhaps they would have. Deep in our hearts, I think we all wanted that to happen. It would have been good for Lisa Marie.

13

"It's too late, baby. He's gone."

MONDAY, AUGUST 15, 1977, was hot and muggy in Memphis, Tennessee. All over the city, air conditioners hummed and while they cooled the air some, they did nothing to relieve the humidity. People went about their daily routines at a slower pace, almost feeling as if they were swimming upstream through the air that hung thick with moisture. It was a typical summer day in the southwest corner of Tennessee right beside the Mississippi River. If you had lived there for long, you had learned to endure it. Chances are you couldn't live there long enough to ever say you enjoyed it.

At Graceland, the air conditioners were on full force. Elvis liked for the house to be kept cool and he kept his room at almost Arctic temperatures. Preparations were being made for the tour that Elvis would start in a couple of days. Clothes had to be packed, final travel arrangements made. Nine-year-old Lisa Marie, who had been visiting her father for a while, was spending her last full day of the visit at Graceland. The next morning, she would be flying home to Priscilla in California. She and her cousins and friends were making the most of the day they had left, running and playing, jumping into the swimming pool to cool off when they became red-faced and sticky in the wet heat. The maids

211

at her father's home would make sure all of her things were packed and ready to go. She didn't have to worry about that.

If Memphis residents had seen the Sunday *Parade* magazine of August 14, they surely were talking about the "Personality Parade" section. It mentioned one of the city's most famous residents. There was a question about the rumor that Elvis was engaged to marry Ginger Alden. The answer *Parade* gave was that "the word in Memphis is that Elvis has fallen deeply in love with Ginger, a stunning brunette and daughter of a retired Army captain." The magazine said that Mrs. Joe Alden, Ginger's mother, "says she will make no official announcement of the couple's engagement or marriage" and that she was leaving the formal announcement up to the couple.

The buzz about Elvis and Ginger at least gave the folks in Memphis something to talk about, something to take their minds off the heat.

During Monday afternoon drive time, radio announcers read the news — as if anyone could think about national or international affairs while they were stuck in motorized pressure cookers all jammed together in little knots of traffic.

Those who were managing to pay attention to the news learned that Congress was debating a balanced budget and the Panama Canal treaty. Scanners to read bar codes and speed up supermarket checkout had gone into the first grocery store in the Southeast — a place called Bruno's in Birmingham, Alabama.

Police still were looking for the "Son of Sam" killer, who randomly and regularly took the lives of young lovers parked in their cars on New York city streets.

First Lady Rosalyn Carter, it was announced, had undergone a "routine gynecological surgical procedure" on August 13th and was celebrating her 50th birthday today, recuperating at the White House.

For those listeners who followed baseball, announcers said, Boston and Minnesota were on top in the American League. Philadelphia and Los Angeles had the lead over in the National League.

And as for the weather, what could they tell those people who were steaming in the Memphis sun? Hang on. There may be some rain on the way and that might break the chokehold the heat and humidity had on the city.

The people who were looking for the coolest place to be in Memphis retreated to the city's theaters. It didn't much matter to them whether they saw *Star Wars* or *The Spy Who Loved Me*. What did matter was that the theater kept its air conditioner on its coldest setting and there was plenty of ice at the refreshment stand.

Mercifully, the sun finally went down that day and brought at least a slight cooling. The people of Memphis put on their coolest pajamas, turned on the fans and went to sleep.

Of course Graceland operated on Elvis Standard Time, which meant that many of the people there were just starting their day when everyone else in Memphis was ending theirs. Some members of Elvis' staff were sitting around the Graceland kitchen when Elvis and his entourage, including Ginger Alden, came down from upstairs and announced that Elvis was going to see the dentist. It was 11 p.m., an odd hour for most people to be getting a filling taken care of, but not at all unusual for Elvis.

His life consisted of doing things at night that other people did during the day. Whether it was shopping, going to a movie or getting a tooth fixed, it happened when there were fewer crowds and not so many people demanding just a moment of Elvis' time, a piece of his attention.

Which was why this group of people were climbing into Elvis' car after the rest of the city had gone to bed. The car pulled away and Elvis was off to the dentist. The staff went back to doing what they had been doing before the group came down and left Graceland.

Elvis came back at about 2 a.m. and made arrangements for a staff member to fly with Lisa Marie back to California. Then he, Ginger and two friends all went over to Graceland's racquetball court to play.

According to *The Death of Elvis: What Really Happened*,

a book by Charles C. Thompson II and James P. Cole (Donna and Edie call this "the autopsy book."), at about 4 a.m., Elvis called his regular physician, Dr. George Nichopoulos, and asked him to call in a prescription for Dilaudid®, a pain killer that Elvis regularly used. Apparently, Elvis had discovered that the tablets he had gotten for pain at the dentist's office contained codeine, a drug to which he was allergic.

The doctor did call in the prescription and it was filled, according to Thompson and Cole.

Back at Graceland, the racquetball game was finishing up about 6 a.m. Elvis and Ginger returned to the house and started getting ready for bed. The rest of Memphis was hitting the snooze buttons on their alarm clocks when Elvis was calling downstairs for a packet of sleeping pills. It wasn't an unusual request. Elvis regularly took pills to help him sleep and pills to help him wake up.

Elvis' Aunt Delta went up to the bedroom at about 8:30 a.m. to take him some water and a copy of the day's newspaper.

Apparently, Elvis called down for packets of pills twice more during the afternoon. Ginger told investigators that she went to sleep shortly after she and Elvis got to the bedroom. Elvis, she said, had told her that he was having trouble getting to sleep and was going into the bathroom to read for a while.

Sometime between 1 and 2 p.m. on August 16, 1977, Ginger woke up and realized that Elvis had not come to bed. Later, she told investigators that when she woke up, she made one, perhaps two, telephone calls. She said she called another young lady who was going on the tour to see what clothes she was packing. She said she may have called her mother as well, but she wasn't sure.

After that, she said, she went to the bathroom door, knocked and called Elvis' name.

There was no answer so Ginger pushed the door open and saw Elvis lying on the carpeted floor, face-down, not moving. She called downstairs and told whoever answered the phone that something was wrong — seriously wrong —

with Elvis. The quiet that had spread over Graceland when Elvis came in that morning to go to bed suddenly was lost in a flurry of noise and activity. Members of Elvis' staff were in the bathroom in minutes, turning the lifeless body over, attempting to perform CPR. Elvis' face was puffy and flushed with uncirculated blood. His tongue had swollen so much it was protruding and he had bitten into it.

Vernon was called and he rushed to Elvis' bedroom. Ginger was sitting on the bed when he came in the door. He asked her what had happened. She looked up at him and shrugged her shoulders.

Ginger called her mother, saying that Elvis was having medical problems.

Someone called for an ambulance. At 2:33 p.m., in Engine House Number 29, Emergency Medical Technicians Charlie Crosby and his partner, Ulysses Jones Jr., jumped into Unit 6 and drove off to answer a call on "someone having difficulty breathing" at 3746 Elvis Presley Boulevard. Crosby recognized the address. He knew they were headed for Graceland. He thought their patient probably would be Vernon Presley. He had made emergency runs to help Elvis' father before. Crosby knew from those experiences that Vernon had problems with his heart and suspected he would be taking the elder Presley to the hospital once again.

On the other hand, he speculated as they drove, it might be another fan who had fainted or been overcome by the heat. The day was another sultry one, thick with heat and humidity. He had made those runs before, too.

What Crosby wasn't prepared for was what actually happened when the ambulance made the turn into the driveway at Graceland. A car met them about halfway up the drive and led them to the front of the house. The two rescue workers followed their guide inside.

Downstairs, about a half dozen people stood around, looking helpless. Crosby caught a quick glimpse of them as he and Jones rushed by. Upstairs, in the bathroom that was their destination, there were another six or so people, all trying to help the person lying on the floor. Dr. Nichopoulos was working on the patient Crosby quickly realized was not Vernon, but Elvis himself.

Crosby and Jones went to work, taking over the CPR and getting their patient ready to transport. They got Elvis onto a stretcher and carried him to the waiting ambulance with Dr. Nichopoulos and two men Crosby didn't recognize following closely. Outside, they put the stretcher in the ambulance and Crosby jumped behind the wheel. Jones and the others climbed in beside the stretcher and the ambulance began its run to Baptist Hospital.

Inside Graceland, things were chaotic. Vernon did the only thing he knew to do, the only thing he thought he could do that might help his son. He picked up the phone and started calling his brother and sisters, asking them to pray for Elvis. Nash was one of the first people he talked to.

She followed her first instincts as well and got her daughters on the phone. Elvis, she had sensed when she heard Vernon's voice, was going to need the prayers of every family member she could contact.

Susie was at her job in a dry cleaning business when her mother called. "She said, 'They've taken Elvis to the hospital. Pray for him. It's pretty bad,' " Susie remembers. "So I started praying. But I just had this feeling that it was too late. I kept praying anyway. I asked if I could go home and they let me go." Susie drove to her house, trying to forget about a dream she had had for the past three nights, but being overcome with the feeling that she now knew what the dream meant.

"I had this dream about a woman who had long, black hair and a long, flowing white robe on," Susie explains. "In the dream, she was coming down the stairs from Elvis' room. When she got to the bottom of the stairs, she just disappeared."

Donna was at home with her children, four-year-old Stacy and Jamie, who was just shy of his first birthday. "Mom called. She was crying and extremely upset," Donna says. "She said, 'Elvis needs our prayers.' She just kept saying, 'It's bad. It's really bad.' She didn't say what was wrong, she just told me to pray and pray hard. She said, 'He's in bad shape and he's...' Then she hung up.

"I didn't have a chance to ask her any questions and I had no idea what the problem was, but I knew something was wrong, so I did what she said."

Donna gathered her sons in their living room and said, "Boys, we have to pray." Jamie, she knew, was too young to understand much of what was going on, but Stacy knelt down beside his mother and folded his hands just the way she did.

"I prayed and prayed as hard as I could," Donna recalls.

At 2:56 p.m., Crosby pulled his ambulance up to the entrance at Memphis' Baptist Hospital and he and Jones unloaded their patient, turning his care over to the emergency room staff. Despite the efforts of the rescue team, Elvis hadn't begun breathing on his own nor had his heart started beating during the trip to the hospital. If the hospital staff was going to be able to help him, it was going to take more than what they had been able to do for him in the ambulance.

A team of physicians and nurses was waiting for their arrival. They went to work, doing all the things they had been trained to do when a patient arrives in this condition. It was quickly evident to them, though, that this patient was beyond resuscitating. He was dead and had been dead for some time. Still, they were hesitant to stop, reluctant to give up on trying. Finally, after about 30 minutes or so, they gave in to the inevitable and stopped efforts to revive their patient. The attending doctor "called it," announcing to the nurse assigned to keep the patient's records the time of death for Elvis Aaron Presley. It was 3:30 p.m. in Memphis.

Dr. Nichopoulos asked Crosby and Jones to take him back to Graceland and wait while he told Vernon that his son was dead. Vernon's heart wasn't good and if anything ever would cause it to stop, it would be the news he was about to get. The doctor also asked the officials at the hospital not to announce Elvis' death until he could talk to Vernon and the rest of the family could be notified.

Crosby and Jones walked into Graceland with Dr. Nichopoulos. The doctor and Vernon went into another room. Crosby and Jones stood, uncomfortable and feeling like intruders on this private moment, in the living room where several family members sat. In the midst of all the adults was a little girl — Lisa Marie.

She sat, Crosby remembered later, crying and very upset. A lady, he told reporters later that day, was holding her and comforting her.

When Dr. Nichopoulos finished talking with Vernon and was assured that Elvis' father wasn't going to need the ambulance, he told the EMTs they could go up and get any equipment they had left in Elvis' bathroom and then it would be okay for them to leave.

Vernon composed himself enough to make some necessary phone calls. Again, Nash's was one of the first numbers he dialed.

She was in the kitchen when Susie walked into the house. "She was crying and she said, 'Honey, Elvis is gone,' " Susie says. "We just hugged and cried."

Donna had been on her knees in her living room ever since her mother's call. "Mom called me back and said, 'It's too late, baby. He's gone,' " Donna says. "I got a neighbor to sit with the kids and I headed for Graceland."

Priscilla was meeting her sister, Michelle, for lunch and a shopping spree that afternoon. When Priscilla dropped by to pick her up, Michelle told her that the people at Graceland were looking frantically for her. Priscilla called and someone there told her the news — Elvis was dead. They were, they told her, sending Elvis' jet, the *Lisa Marie*, to pick her up and bring her to Memphis.

Lisa Marie was old enough to understand at least part of what was going on at Graceland. She probably didn't understand what was happening to her grandfather. He was crying, upset, yet trying to rush around and get things done. Minnie was trying to help him, but she, too, was weeping, almost unable to move. Relatives were arriving, red-eyed and appearing to be on the verge of collapse. If Lisa Marie didn't understand anything else, she surely knew that something had happened at Graceland the likes of which she never had seen before.

Someone finally told her what had happened to her father or she figured it out on her own. Either way, it was news with which it was hard for a nine-year-old to cope. Her father wasn't there, the adults she usually depended on at Graceland were in no shape to help her and her mother was in the air, getting to her as quickly as she could but not there beside her yet. She turned to someone else she had known and cared for. Lisa Marie placed a phone call to Linda Thompson, the young woman Elvis had dated for several years. When Linda answered the phone, she heard the young voice that she recognized at once.

"My daddy's dead," the youngster sobbed into the phone, "and nobody knows."

After Lisa Marie called Linda, Nash took over the phone. She called Edie's home in Birmingham, where she knew her cousin was recuperating from major surgery. Edie, discharged from the hospital just the day before, answered.

"She said, 'Edie, if you're not sitting down, you need to,'" Edie remembers. "And I said, 'Is it Minnie?' She said, 'No, Edie, it's Elvis. He's dead.' I could hear Lisa Marie in the background. She was crying and saying, 'Aunt Nash, my daddy's dead!'

"Nash said, 'Can you come?' I told her I'd have to ask my doctor and I did, but he wouldn't let me go."

It was 4 p.m. in Memphis. Vernon had told all the people he thought he had to tell right away. Some of Elvis' staff members were still out running errands they had to do before the tour, so they hadn't heard. And he hadn't contacted all the relatives in Tupelo, but he and the family members and friends who had joined in to help had called everyone they could. Vernon knew he couldn't keep the news from getting out much longer. He gave the okay for the hospital to make the announcement.

A spokesman for Baptist Hospital confirmed the worst fears of the people who had gotten wind of the fact that Elvis had been taken to the hospital. Elvis Presley, he said, had died at 3:30 p.m. An autopsy was being performed at the request of Vernon Presley and the results would be released at a press conference later.

Reporters rushed for phones. Radio stations broke into their regular programming. Television stations carried the news. At one mall, a member of Elvis' staff was picking up some clothes that Elvis would need on his tour. He had been out of touch with Graceland all day, taking care of last-minute details for the trip. He looked across the mall into a shoe store. The employee there was sobbing as if her heart would break. Obviously she was in distress and needed a shoulder to lean on. He went into the store and asked what was wrong. When the shoe store employee told him that Elvis was dead, he went into a rage, screaming that she should never say anything like that. He was a member of Elvis' staff, he told her. If the singer were dead, he certainly would know about it.

Be that as it may, the woman told him, the radio station she was listening to had just announced that Elvis had died. The staff member sprinted to his car, jumped in and headed for Graceland. Along the way, he tried several different radio stations. All that he could get on any of them was Elvis' music. Even without hearing an official announcement, he knew then it was true. Elvis was gone.

Making a phone call in, out of or to Memphis suddenly became impossible. Telephone companies are equipped to handle lots of calls every day. They just weren't equipped to handle the volume of calls in Memphis that day. As the news went out over the radio and television, people in Memphis began calling one another and calling relatives and friends who didn't live in the city. In a matter of minutes, the phone lines were hopelessly congested and, like cars in some huge traffic jam, all the messages were clogged up in Memphis exchange switches. The calls ground to a halt and telephone communications stopped for a few minutes to let the telephone company catch up with the demand. Everybody had to share the news with someone else. Sharing the grief was the only way to make it bearable. After a while, the connections were re-established and once again, the calling began.

When Elvis' employee got to Graceland from the mall, he found that several of Elvis' relatives already had arrived and others were on the way. It's another Southern tradition. Just as relatives gather to welcome new family members, they gather to say good-bye to those they've lost. Houses may burst at the seams, filled with generation after generation, but that doesn't stop family members from arriving. Whatever they have to face, they face together. They present a united front against overwhelming sorrow and lean on one another for strength and comfort.

Donna arrived at Graceland, rushing in the back door and heading straight for Minnie's room. "I knew she would be terribly upset," Donna remembers, "and I wanted to be with her. I knew all the family would be there."

She got sidetracked from her destination, however, when she got to the hallway leading to her grandmother's room. There, Vernon sat, talking on the telephone. "He was totally devastated. He looked like the life had been drained out of him, like he hadn't eaten or slept for a month. My heart felt as though it would burst and I only could imagine the pain and suffering he was feeling.

"I knelt down in front of him," Donna says, "and we cried and hugged each other. I kissed him on the cheek, tears were streaming down his face and with each breath he took you almost could hear his heart breaking." After a few more minutes with her Uncle Vernon, she went on to her grandmother's room.

"Mom and Aunt Delta were in there with Grandma," she says. "Everyone was crying and upset. Elvis had been such an influence on all of our lives and now he was gone. It just didn't seem real. It was a nightmare and we just wanted to wake up. Grandma was so hurt, but I knew that day where my mom got her strength."

When they no longer could bear to see their family in such grief, Nash and Earl left for a few minutes. They walked over to the home of Tish Henley, Dr. Nichopoulos' nurse, who always was on duty at Graceland. "Mom told me she looked at Tish and said, 'Tish, what happened?' " Donna says. "She said that Tish just answered, 'I hope to God he had a heart attack.' " Sometime during that awful day Nash told Donna what Tish had said, but Donna didn't think much about it at the time. She was too tired, too sad to wonder much about what the nurse had meant. Ms. Henley's words would come back to her, though, a couple of years later, when she looked back on the day Elvis died.

At one point, Dan Warlick, an investigator for the Shelby County Medical Examiner's Office, arrived to secure evidence necessary any time someone dies at home or any place other than a hospital. He would have to take some pictures, make some notes and maybe ask some questions. Warlick, though professional, tried to be sensitive when he found himself in these situations. After all, he was coming into a house where a family had lost someone they loved. He needed to do his job, but he needed to do it with compassion.

Warlick rang the front doorbell and was let into Graceland. As he stood in the entrance hall, he glanced to his right. There was a little girl sitting there. Warlick realized quickly that she looked like a miniature version of Elvis. It had to be Lisa Marie. She was crying. Warlick tried not to get emotionally involved when he went out to gather evidence like this. But it was hard not to feel for this child. The thought ran through his head as he watched a lady dressed in white comfort Lisa Marie that this little girl, Elvis' only child, had lost her daddy. It reminded him that no matter whose home he was gathering evidence from, he still was dealing with people.

He walked down the hall and saw Vernon Presley talking on the phone. "My baby is dead," he was telling someone on the other end. Then he started crying, sobbing so hard that he almost fell down. Usually Warlick wouldn't have let their tears get to him, but he only had been in Graceland a few minutes and already he had encountered a child who had just lost her father and a father who had just lost his son.

When Priscilla arrived, Lisa Marie had gone outside and was riding around in her golf cart. Looking so much like her father, she created almost a flashback to the day Nash had found Elvis riding on a golf cart across the grounds at

Graceland, just taking advantage of the chance to be by himself.

There might have been some people who didn't think Lisa Marie was being properly respectful to her father. But her family knew what was going on. They thought what she was doing was fine.

"That was her way of dealing with it. She just had to get out for a while. She was suffocating," Donna explains. "A nine-year-old girl — her daddy's just died and her mama hadn't gotten there yet. Even though there was family there, they were dealing with their own grief. What's a child to do?"

Meanwhile upstairs, according to Thompson and Cole, Warlick was discovering that there really wasn't much evidence left to gather. The bed in Elvis' room had been made up, the bathroom cleaned. One of the maids, he was told, had come in and done it after the ambulance left with Elvis. Even with all the cleaning, Warlick was able to determine one thing. Elvis had vomited when he fell face-forward in the bathroom that day. Warlick made some pictures and left.

Elvis' fans all over the nation were finding their own ways to deal with his death as well. They had begun calling radio stations, crying as they told disc jockeys how much Elvis had meant to them, requesting his songs. They had swamped record stores throughout America, buying Elvis' recordings as fast as the cash registers could ring them up. The manager at a Buffalo, New York, record store, one of the largest in the nation, said the stock at the store was depleted within a few hours of the announcement of Elvis' death. A store in Florida sold $700 worth of Elvis' records in a few hours. United Press International was reporting by that night that stores everywhere were looking for supplies to refill their stock for the next day's business.

Airlines' reservations numbers were ringing off the hook with Elvis fans calling to see if they could get a flight to Memphis. Quickly, all the available seats filled up and Delta Airlines added two more flights from Atlanta to try to accommodate more fans.

In Tupelo, Mississippi, some of Elvis' family members were gathering at the house where he was born. They came together just to talk and to think about the little boy who had lived here and the man he had grown up to be. They needed a central place to come together and mourn with one another. They chose the simple shotgun house that often was described as being on the "wrong side of the tracks" in Tupelo. For now, though, it was home once again to them. They could sit there and be with one another even though no Presley lived there now. Fans from in and around Tupelo came there, too, looking for a place where they could feel near Elvis. Fans and family were joined there by tourists who, by coincidence, had scheduled their visit to the singer's birthplace on what would turn out to be an unforgettable day. Many of the visitors and fans brought flowers and left them in front of the house. Before the sun set in Tupelo, there was a bank of flowers covering the porch and part of the yard.

Flags in Tupelo flew at half-staff in honor of the city's native son. Back in Memphis, flags all over the city were being lowered to half-staff to salute the man who had made the town his home.

Outside the fence at Graceland, Elvis fans who were in Memphis or could get there quickly had begun to gather. There wasn't much else they could do but stand there and stare at the house. It didn't really look that much different, still the same house, still the same grounds, still the same gates. But everything for them had changed. Elvis wasn't at home there anymore. Never again would they see his motorcycle or his automobile pull out of the gates and catch a quick glimpse of the singer. Never again could they fantasize that he came down to the front wall at night and read the messages they left for him. It just wouldn't ever be the same.

The people looking out of Graceland at the crowds were thinking the same thing. And it was beginning to dawn on them that this wasn't going to be an ordinary funeral. They had grown accustomed, over the years, to losing much of their privacy because of being related to Elvis. They just never had thought much about really personal moments like this

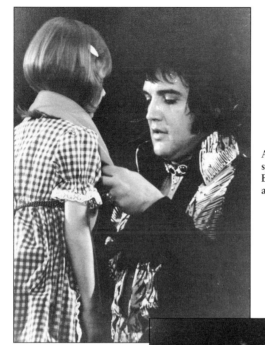

A young fan receives
special gifts from
Elvis -- a ring, a scarf
and a hug.

This photograph of Vernon was taken in September 1976 as he drove out of the gates of Graceland.

Delta reflects on her memories of nephew Elvis.

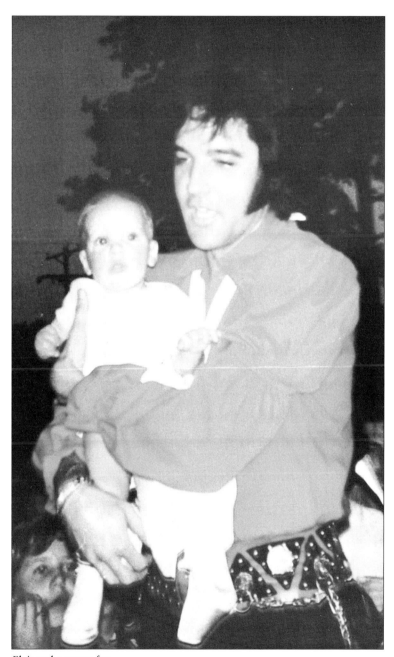

Elvis and a young fan.

Elvis' 1977 Birmingham concert. (Photo by Axford's Photography.)

The living room/music room at Graceland the way it was the day Elvis died. After their deaths, Elvis, Vernon and Dodger lay in state in the open doorway.

At Elvis' gravesite in 1979. From left, Jimmy Gambill and
Dena Gambill (Patsy's son and daughter), Buddy, Lisa Marie,
Donna and friends.

In 1985 Elvis' friend Eddie Fadal sent Nash this picture which years earlier had
been made of him and Elvis. The inscription on the back is, "Faithfully your
friend always through Christ, Love, Eddie Fadal, 1985."

Christmas at Graceland, 1992,
seven months before Delta's
death. From left, Susie, Donna,
Nash and Delta.

Susie, Nash
and Donna
vacationing
in Florida.

Nash and daughter Susie at an Elvis charity function.

Nash shows off a scarf from Paris, a gift from a fan.

Donna on a vacation in Maui, Hawaii, in 1995.

Donna's son Stacy Aaron (Elvis' namesake) with his bride, Leigh Ann, on their wedding day, May 20, 1995.

Elvis' cousins Jamie and Stacy on Stacy's wedding day.

Elvis' stepbrother Rick
Stanley, Edie, and Charlie
Hodge with TV talk show
host Sally Jessy Raphael.

Photo shot from
Donna's modeling
portfolio, 1989.

Donna vacationing in
Panama City, Florida,
in 1982.

"Dr. Casey" and Edie as "Dr. Porter" appearing
on daytime drama *As the World Turns*.

Advertising firm president and entertainer Edie Hand, 1986.

Edie in New York for opening of *Elvis: A Rockin' Remembrance*.

Edie and Lifetime Cable Network CEO Doug McCormick.

Edie and Marie Osmond, backstage at Country Music Association Awards, 1992.

Country music group Alabama joins Edie and space campers in Huntsville, Alabama, for EVE Foundation kickoff.

Edie and her son, Linc, in 1991.

Edie with country music singer Tanya Tucker and Ms. Tucker's daughter, Presley.

Entertainer George Lindsey with Edie.

Edie's impersonation of Phyllis Diller. Of all the roles Elvis saw Edie do, this was his favorite.

Edie as "Pearl," the role she popular- ized in syndicated commercials.

Elvis' entertainer cousins, The Hacker Brothers: Ace, Anthony and Hartty.

Elvis' cousins, entertainers Alice and Joey Coleman.
(Courtesy of Judy Coleman Martino.)

Elvis' second cousin Jackie Coleman, who has taught music in Indiana for
more than 30 years.

Susie and Nash, in left rear, at an Elvis fan convention in State of Washington.

The front of Graceland, 1972. Fans were known to try to climb massive oaks near the mansion.

Dodger's grave immediately after her burial at Graceland.

Buddy placing floral arrangements on Elvis' grave, 1980.

Elvis the performer.

one — none of them had really ever thought about Elvis' funeral. He was too young for them to spend much time on such thoughts. Still, here it was. And it was becoming obvious that their grieving was going to be done in a very public forum.

"You can imagine how hard it was for all of us with Elvis' picture, music, movies all over the TV and the radio," Donna says. "You couldn't turn on the TV or radio without it being covered by the media. It's hard enough to grieve, to go through losing a loved one, without everyone talking about it, saying this and saying that. It was just like people were coming out of the woodwork. Always cameras around, taking pictures, flashing this, flashing that."

Planning the funeral was going to take some extra thought. Vernon, Nash, Delta, Minnie and Vester sat down and started talking about arrangements. Donna stood behind Minnie's chair, ready to offer her support and suggestions, trying to take it all in.

The funeral should be private, of course — everyone agreed on that. And the burial would have to be somewhere that could be made secure. What kind of service should they have? Music? Who would deliver it? What ministers should they ask to conduct the funeral? The questions just kept coming.

They had to make some decisions right away. The seamless copper coffin they ordered would have to be flown in from Oklahoma City. They chose a blanket of red rosebuds to put on top of the casket. Roses had been one of Elvis' favorite flowers. They were what he would have wanted.

Elvis had closets full of clothes at Graceland. Which should they chose to bury him in? After some discussion, they chose a white suit, blue shirt and white tie. They chose a ring bearing Elvis' "TCB" ("Taking Care of Business") motto for him to wear. The clothes were sent over to the funeral home. But the family still had other decisions to make.

They chose Rev. C.W. Bradley, minister of the Wooddale Church of Christ, a friend of the family for more than a decade, to lead the funeral service. Assisting him would be

Rev. Rex Humbard of Akron, Ohio. It was 1 a.m. when Vernon went to call Rev. Bradley and ask him if he would be available to conduct the services.

Then came the question of music. Once again, the family members gathered to discuss that. They would ask Kathy Westmoreland, who had been one of Elvis' back-up singers for years, to sing something. "I said, 'Uncle Vernon, what about including "How Great Thou Art?" It was one of Elvis' favorites and one he had recorded,' " Donna says. Vernon, who never forgot that Elvis had fans and friends, spent a little while longer making phone calls, trying to anticipate problems that might arise. There was a Shriners' convention going on in Memphis and almost every hotel room was filled. Vernon called a few and asked if there was any way they could make some rooms available to family members, friends and members of the press. The hotels began asking Shriners if they could double up and vacate some rooms. As many as could helped out and a few rooms were made ready for people coming to Memphis for the funeral.

With all of that done, the members of Elvis Presley's family went to bed. They probably wouldn't sleep well, but they would make the effort. The lights were turned out at Graceland. What seemed like the longest day any of them had lived finally, mercifully, came to an end.

Outside, the fans kept their vigil. While Elvis' family tried to get some rest, they would be the watchers in the night. It was the last thing they could do for Elvis.

Wednesday morning didn't bring any relief from the sadness or from the heat and humidity. By now, there were thousands of Elvis' fans outside Graceland. They sweltered in the sticky warmth, just looking at the mansion, wondering what would happen next.

Inside, the people were getting ready for what would be one of the worst moments they would have to face. Elvis' body would be brought home to Graceland that afternoon. They knew intellectually that Elvis was dead, but when the hearse brought him home and they saw him, their hearts would have to admit it as well. It was going to be a long, difficult day on the hill.

"Someone has said that Uncle Vernon had Elvis brought back to Graceland for the funeral because he was observing a tradition that was established by poor people who didn't have the money to have the viewing at the funeral home," Donna says. "That's just not true. It's a Southern tradition, all right, but it doesn't have to do with money. They bring the body home because that's the place where that person lived. It was his home. There's not a more appropriate place for a person to be than the place he lived in and loved."

Besides, Donna points out, "Uncle Vernon knew that security and crowd control were going to be a problem even at Graceland where they were somewhat prepared for it. It would be beyond the scope of any funeral home to handle that many people who wanted to get in. He had to do what was best for the public, for the funeral home, for his family and for Elvis."

All that day, the fans waited outside Graceland. The police asked for — and got — help from the National Guard and the State Troopers. It wasn't necessarily that the fans were being rowdy or irreverent, it was just that there were so many of them. They also called on the Red Cross and local ambulance companies for assistance. In the heat and crush of the crowd, people were fainting, collapsing from a combination of emotion and heat prostration. They needed medical attention. Rescue workers and Red Cross personnel carried people onto the grass of Graceland all day, stretching them out, cooling them off, giving them something to drink.

Even the most tired, hottest fan took note, however, when the white hearse pulled into the gates and up the driveway. Fans had been sending flower arrangements to Graceland all day long. The florists of Memphis had gone through all their stock and started directing callers to flower shops in other cities. All around the front porch at the mansion, arrangements — from simple bud vases with single roses to elaborate creations spelling out Elvis' name or forming a spotted hound dog with a guitar-shaped tag — sat waiting for the arrival of the body.

244 ELVIS: PRECIOUS MEMORIES

The men from the funeral home stepped out of the hearse, opened the back door and slid the copper casket out. Slowly, they carried it into Graceland. In the living room, they arranged it on the bier they had brought, opened it and left. Elvis was home with his family. It was the moment they had spent their day anticipating and dreading.

"Uncle Vernon, Sandy (Sandy Miller, Vernon's nurse and fiancee), Grandma and I went in to see him," Donna recalls. "I thought Uncle Vernon would faint. Sandy was supporting him. I was supporting Grandma. Uncle Vernon just cried and said over and over again, 'My baby's gone.' Then he said, 'Son, Daddy will be with you soon.' It almost was prophetic. Twenty-two months later, Uncle Vernon was gone."

Priscilla took Lisa Marie up to the casket. "Daddy died," she told her daughter. "He's gone to be with God."

Slowly, the rest of the family made their way in, each member lost in his own thoughts. Nash was thinking of the last time she saw Elvis alive. It had been two weeks before he died and Minnie was very sick:

> Dr. Nick was upstairs with Elvis, so Delta called upstairs and told Elvis that Mom was sick. He and the doctor came down to her room. Elvis asked Mom if she minded if I prayed for her. I already had, but he didn't know it. Mom said she wanted me to pray for her again, so Elvis knelt down beside her bed along with me. We held hands and prayed for her. As I stood up, I looked down at his hands (He had put them on the bed beside Mom.) I noticed something special about his hands. What I didn't know was that two weeks later, I would see those hands folded on his chest in his casket.

The sight that greeted Donna when she walked up to that open coffin is forever etched on her memory and it's what she calls upon when she hears rumors that Elvis isn't dead. "How do I answer those people?" she says. "I would say they would have had to be there to see the look on Uncle

Vernon's face, to see Grandma and to see Lisa Marie. Even if you could imagine that Elvis would pull something like faking his death, you would know he couldn't have done that to those people. He loved them more than life itself. He would never have put them through that, never have hurt them that way. He just couldn't have done it to them. Yes, Elvis is dead. He died that day in August, 1977. Believe me, his family would be the first people to wish it wasn't so. But it is. There was no hoax. No tricks were pulled. It wasn't a wax dummy in that coffin, there weren't rocks to weight it down. It was Elvis. He's gone. You can't imagine how much it hurts the family to see those kinds of stories in tabloids. Try to think how you would feel if it were someone you loved. When you're standing in line in a grocery store and see these headlines about how he called Bill Clinton just the other day, you would wish it could be true. But he isn't alive, he isn't calling President Clinton or meeting secretly with Lisa Marie about her career. And it still hurts after all these years to read things like that."

"He could have pulled it off," Nash once told a reporter. "He had a lot of power, a lot of money. He was a popular man. But he wouldn't pull a stunt like that. We wish he were alive, but that's just not true. Can you imagine? Just think about the heartache that Vernon and Lisa Marie went through."

In the midst of his grief, Vernon thought about Elvis' fans — these were the people who had made Elvis what he was. Without them and their loyalty, Elvis wouldn't have made it to the top. They deserved a proper chance to say good-bye to the singer as well. What Vernon, like Elvis, didn't comprehend fully were the huge numbers of people who were Elvis fans. When Vernon had it announced that Elvis' body would be placed in the foyer at Graceland for the fans to come by and view, he had no idea how many people would get in line for that opportunity. At 3 p.m., the doors of Graceland were opened to the fans. Vernon originally had planned for the viewing to go on for two hours. One look outside Graceland confirmed that two hours wasn't going to be enough time. Thousands of people — many of whom had waited all night long — stood outside. Vernon decided to leave the mansion open to fans until 6:30 p.m. At 6 p.m., there still were 10,000 people in line and between 20,000 and 25,000 had viewed the body. Police estimated that between 50,000 and 100,000 people had been outside Graceland that day. The sheer magnitude of the numbers confirmed what Elvis' family had known — the grief over the loss of Elvis was something they were going to have to share with the world.

At 6:30 p.m. on the night of August 17, twelve police officers slowly pushed the gates of Graceland closed. Police barricades went up to move the crowd back and the fans began to leave. By late that night, only about 400 were left. Once again, a relative quiet fell over Graceland and Elvis' family tried again to sleep.

At about 3:30 a.m., the peace was shattered by the sound of sirens. A drunk driver had hit three young ladies standing outside Graceland. Two of the teenagers were killed instantly. The other was taken to the hospital in critical condition. The car narrowly missed a police officer. Other officers stopped the car and arrested the driver. Fans outside the mansion were horrified by the accident, at a loss about how to help. The two girls who died were from Louisiana. The third, now destined to have a long stay in a Memphis hospital, was from Missouri. It didn't take long for Elvis fans to come through for the injured girl just as they always had for Elvis. Before the day was out, The Graceland Fan Club had arranged a fund-raising drive to help pay expenses for Tammy Baiter, whose birthday was the same day as Elvis', and her family.

A few hours after the accident, the sun came up in Memphis. It was the day of Elvis Presley's funeral. No one had thought it was possible, but it was steamier on Thursday than it had been on Tuesday and Wednesday. A light mist had fallen for a while the day before, but it did nothing to clear the air of its overload of moisture and it brought no cooling with it.

The crowd began to gather in front of Graceland, this time spilling over down the street and lining the path the hearse would take as it wound its way to Forest Hill Cemetery later in the day. Others went directly to the cemetery and waited there. One hundred vans from florists throughout the area began pulling up the drive at Graceland and loading the floral arrangements. Florists had filled more than 3,000 orders for flowers and the names on the cards ranged from fans who never had met Presley personally to entertainers — Glen Campbell, the Carpenters, Elton John, Donna Fargo — to city and state officials — Gov. Ray Blanton and the Memphis Police Association. The vans began moving in at 9 a.m. They carried the last arrangement to the cemetery at 1 p.m., just in time for the limousines that would take Elvis' immediate family and the celebrity guests to the cemetery to start pulling into the driveway.

Inside Graceland, the family readied itself for the funeral services. Susie looked out at the crowds and thought how the day almost had taken on a zoo-like atmosphere. "We were really hurting," she remembers, "and there were so many people. It was really hard on us. But it was gratifying to know so many people loved Elvis."

Elvis' friends and family began to gather at Graceland for the 2 p.m. private funeral that was to take place in the music room/living room. Ann-Margret, Elvis' one-time leading lady and close friend, arrived with her husband, Roger Smith. Actor George Hamilton, himself a Memphis native, came to say good-bye to his friend Elvis. Their presence was touching to members of the singer's family.

"I always had respected their talent," Donna says, "but I learned a new, deeper respect for them at the funeral. They were very quiet, very subdued. They weren't there to show off. They weren't there to be seen. They were there to pay their respects to a man whom they loved and admired because they were dear friends of his.

"It really made me feel so good to see these people, people I had seen on the screen and listened to on records and tapes, and to see how much they loved and admired and respected

Elvis. It really meant a lot to me. I appreciated it. The entire family appreciated it."

Just as Elvis' friends had gathered to pay their respects and to say good–bye, so had his family. That's all the family was there for, Donna says. "I've read how some people said we all swooped down on Graceland like a bunch of vultures waiting for the will to be read to see what we got. That's not true. We all knew what was in Elvis' will. Everything was going to Lisa Marie eventually and that's how it should be. Elvis was her daddy and what he had should be hers."

"Some of the things I've read made us sound like the Beverly Hillbillies, driving up in a truck and ready to load everything in Graceland up and tie Minnie on top in a rocking chair," Edie says. "That's just not the way it was. If we had been half as bad as some people made us look, there wouldn't be anything left at Graceland to display."

Elvis' family wasn't busily checking to see where the good china was stored, they insist, but quietly going about the process of mourning. They would have traded in every piece of good china just to have Elvis back with them. But that wasn't going to be and Elvis' funeral was about to begin.

The air conditioners at Graceland churned away, but they were fighting a losing battle against the heat outside and the crowd inside. Two hundred people were invited to the funeral. Chairs were set up for them and, as they took their seats, hand fans were given out in an attempt to keep them more comfortable. They waved the fans and stirred the hot air around, but the weather and the emotion made it almost impossible to breathe.

At 2 p.m., Vernon and the other family members were seated and the music began. Rev. Bradley stood and began to speak. He talked about Elvis' life and his devotion to family and friends:

"Words do not take away from a man's life and words do not add to a man's life in the sight of God. Though I will make several personal observations regarding Elvis, and from them seek to encourage us, it is not my purpose to try to eulogize him. This is being done by thousands throughout the world.

"We are here to honor the memory of a man loved by millions. Elvis can serve as an inspiring example of the great potential of one human being who has a strong desire and unfailing determination. From total obscurity, Elvis rose to world fame. His name is a household word in every nook and corner of this earth. Though idolized by millions and forced to be protected from the crowds, Elvis never lost his desire to stay in close touch with humanity.

"Vernon told my wife and me one day while we ate and talked together that he constantly had stressed to Elvis that he must never forget his humble beginning. And I don't believe that he did. This could be seen in his regular contributions to so many who needed help. Truly I believe Elvis did not want to lose contact with humanity.

"In a society that has talked so much about the generation gap, the closeness of Elvis and his father and his constant dependence upon Vernon's counsel was heartwarming to observe. Elvis never forgot his family. In a thousand ways he showed his great love for them.

"In a world where so many pressures are brought upon us to lose our identity, to be lost in the masses, Elvis dared to be different...Elvis was different and no one else ever can be exactly like him. Wherever and whenever his voice was heard, everybody knew that was Elvis Presley.

"But Elvis was a frail human being. And he would be the first to admit his weakness. Perhaps because of his rapid rise to fame and fortune, he was thrown into temptations that some never experience. Elvis would not want anyone to think that he had no flaws or faults. But now that he's gone, I find it more helpful to remember his good qualities and I hope you do, too.

"We are here to offer comfort and encouragement to Elvis' family. There is much encouragement in all the beautiful flowers sent by loving hands and hearts around the world. There is much encouragement in the presence of so many who have crowded into our city in addition to those here. And also from knowing that literally millions throughout the earth have their hearts turned in this direction at this hour. There also is much encouragement from the beautiful music. But the greatest comfort and strength come from knowing there is a God in heaven who looks down upon us with love and compassion and who says, 'I will never leave you or forsake you.'

"As the words of a hymn by S.M.T. Henry tell us,
'I know my heavenly Father knows
The storms that would oppose
For He can drive the clouds away
And turn my darkness into day.

'I know my heavenly Father knows
The balm I need to soothe my woes
And with His touch of love divine
He heals this wounded soul of mine.

'I know my heavenly Father knows
How frail I am to meet my foes
But He my cause will e'er defend
Uphold and keep me to the end.'

"We are reminded that we, too, soon must depart this life. The Bible vividly emphasizes the brevity and uncertainty of life. Once when King Saul was chasing David across the country, David said, 'There is but a step between me and death.' And none of us knows when he shall take that step.

"Elvis died at 42. Some of you may not live to be that old but it's not how long we live that's really important, but how we live. If we reject the Bible, then personally I find that life has no real meaning. The Bible teaches that God's plans and purposes for man culminated in the death and resurrection of His son on a cross. Jesus lives today. And because He lives, through Him we can have hope of life beyond the grave.

" 'Oh death, where is thy sting? Oh grave where is thy victory? The sting of death is sin and the strength of sin is

MEMPHIS-SHELBY COUNTY HEALTH DEPARTMENT   313

BURIAL PERMIT

THIS PERMIT MUST ACCOMPANY BODY TO CEMETERY

FULL NAME OF DECEASED *Elvis Presley*

AGE *42* SEX *M* COLOR *W* PLACE OF DEATH *Baptist*

DATE OF DEATH *8-16* 19 *77* CAUSE OF DEATH

CEMETERY *Forest Hill M.T. Maus* PLACE *Mph, Tn*

UNDERTAKER *Mph. F. H. Union* ADDRESS *Mph, Tn*

——————————— PERMIT ———————————

A CERTIFICATE OF DEATH HAVING BEEN FILED AS REQUIRED BY LAW. PERMISSION IS HEREBY GIVEN TO *Mph. F. H. Union* UNDERTAKER. TO BURY THE BODY AS STATED.

DATE *8-17* 19 *77* REGISTRATION DIST. No. *791* SIGNATURE *George Johnny*

HEALTH OFFICER

——————— CEMETERY AUTHORITY SHALL FILL OUT SPACE BELOW ———————

BODY WAS BURIED ON *Aug 18* 19 *77* IN *Forest Hill Cemetery* CEMETERY

PLACE *Memphis Tennessee* SIGNATURE (SEXTON) *R Davis*

☞ THIS PERMIT NOT TO BE USED FOR CREMATION. DISINTERMENT. ☜
TRANSPORTATION BY COMMON CARRIER OR REMOVAL FROM THE STATE

Burial permit used for burial of Elvis Presley.

the law. But thanks be to God, which giveth us the victory through our Lord Jesus Christ.' (I Corinthians 15:55-58)

"Thus, today, I hold up Jesus Christ to all of us. And challenge each of you to commit your heart and your life to Him. May these moments of quiet and thoughtful meditation and reflection on Elvis' life serve to help us reflect upon our own lives and to re-examine our own lives. And may these moments help us to reset our compasses. All of us sometimes get going in the wrong direction."

"It was a beautiful service, but it was heartbreaking, too," Donna recalls.

There were more words and more music and then the hour-long service was over. Elvis' family and friends got up and went out to the waiting cars.

"That's another thing that has been written about us," Donna says. "One person wrote that we had a big fight inside Graceland right after the funeral about who was going to ride in what limousine. That's not true. We knew that Uncle Vernon and Sandy were going to ride in a limo and that some of the guests were going to, but why should we? We all had fine cars, most of them given to us by Elvis. We just rode in them over to the cemetery. The Presley family didn't need limousines. They were for the guests. That was clear from the start and there was no argument about seating in them. Not ever."

The air in Memphis was unusually still and everything was quiet as Vernon made his way to his limousine and sat down inside. Ginger Alden and her mother were riding in the limo behind Vernon's and they went to get in it. While they still were standing outside the car, the quiet was shattered by a deafening "CRACK." A huge limb fell off a nearby tree and crashed to the ground, brushing the Alden limousine and almost hitting Ginger. "It was eerie," Donna remembers.

Once everyone had gotten into their cars, the procession pulled out of the grounds at Graceland. Elvis had been inside the house he loved for the last time. A police escort was waiting and the lead limo, followed by the white hearse, fell in behind it, going down Elvis Presley Boulevard. The rest of the cars followed. The policemen who would stay behind to guard the gates at Graceland raised their hands in a final salute. Fans lined both sides of the street. It took almost an hour for the procession to make the 2-1/2 mile trip to Forest Hill Cemetery. The hearse drove through the cemetery gates at 4 p.m. and pulled up to the cemetery's mausoleum, not far from Gladys Presley's grave.

"I remember the drive," Donna says. "We were following the hearse with Elvis' body and going to the cemetery. People lined the streets all the way from Graceland to the cemetery. There wasn't an inch of space between them. It was a beautiful thing to see. These people, they were not Elvis' family, not in the blood sense, but they were Elvis' family in every other sense. They took that man to their hearts, to their lives, to their homes and he became a part of each and every one of them. It was totally incredible.

"I'll never forget that. It warms your heart just to think about it. All those people were holding up signs that said, 'Elvis, We Love You' and 'Gone, But Not Forgotten.' It was a beautiful, beautiful thing to see. It truly was spectacular to see how much love was generated by that one man. To see how he inspired people to show that kind of love and affection for him. I've never seen anything else like it."

Now Elvis' fans had seen him on his final journey. The choice of the mausoleum was another consequence of Elvis' fame. Everyone knew that he would have chosen to be buried beside his mother. But Vernon knew he had to choose a place that would be secure. The mausoleum was the only logical place. Earlier that day, Wilbert McGhee, the cemetery employee who would wave at Elvis when the singer came to visit his mother's grave, had overseen the opening of the crypt where Elvis' body would be placed.

It seemed odd to McGhee, who was in his sixties, that he would be opening a crypt for someone who barely was forty. And it made him sad. He and Elvis had sort of developed this friendship as they waved to one another across the cemetery. He was going to miss that.

Elvis' family and friends walked into the mausoleum chapel and listened as the ministers said a few final words. After that, his friends filed out slowly and left the family alone with the body for a while. Vernon walked up to the casket, placed his hand on it and just stood there, not saying anything, alone with his thoughts. As he turned to leave, he stumbled slightly and Sandy stepped up to help him. Vernon and his family left the mausoleum and walked through a path made for them in the floral arrangements, back to their cars, back to Graceland.

After Elvis' family left, workmen moved into the mausoleum and began sealing the crypt that held his body. It was sealed with a double slab of concrete, then with marble. For the time being, the marble was blank. Later, the name Elvis Aaron Presley would be added to mark the singer's crypt.

Always thinking of Elvis' fans, Vernon asked that the flower arrangements be taken apart and individual flowers handed out to the fans who had waited the past three days in Memphis to have one last chance to say good-bye, to share their memories of Elvis.

Elvis' family was back together at Graceland, just as they had been so many times during his life, but things never would be the same. Everything on the hill had changed. Being there, getting on with life, was going to be very difficult for all of them.

14

"It was different being
on the hill after Elvis died."

"THE ONLY UNHAPPY TIMES I can remember having at Graceland were the months right after a member of our family died," Donna says. Graceland definitely was an unhappy place for Elvis' family members after his death. Someone who had been very dear to them no longer was there. What was the point of having fireworks fights if Elvis wasn't there to set the house on fire? Why play practical jokes on one another when you knew that you weren't going to hear his deep laughter? "It was different being on the hill after Elvis died," Donna explains.

It was hard to stay focused, to get your job done. Yet Graceland still was the family home. The work still had to be done there. And all of the fans' expressions of sympathy and loss had to be acknowledged.

Elvis' family was finding that it was hard to gather themselves and go on, to try to put things behind them when they constantly saw Elvis' picture on the television and in the newspaper, when they heard his music everywhere.

"It took me two years to be able to listen to an Elvis recording without crying," Donna says. "One night, Buddy took me out to this place where we went to dance. They had video screens all around the ceiling. All of a sudden, Elvis'

'American Trilogy' starts playing and I look up at the screens
and they are showing the funeral procession leaving
Graceland. I had to get out of there. It was hard."

And then there were the tabloids. Nash remembered the
one she disliked the most:

> *Delta and I went into a local grocery and as I
> walked by the magazine rack the first thing that caught
> my eye was a scandal sheet with a picture of Elvis
> lying in his casket. I told Delta to look and we both
> stood there in shock. Later we found out someone
> had worn a tiny camera into the house when Elvis'
> body lay in state there in the entrance hall at
> Graceland, took a picture and sold it to the maga-
> zine.*

"I think that one hurt the most," Donna says. "The person who did that had to know how painful it would be for
us, especially for Lisa Marie."

Often, ministers and television evangelists were as hurtful as tabloid editors, Nash remembered:

> *When Elvis died, a minister called me and said,
> "Elvis was spoiled, but that wasn't his fault, it was
> his mother and daddy's fault." Those were not com-
> forting words.*
>
> *Right after Elvis passed away, Vernon was watch-
> ing television (I think it was a Sunday morning). Some
> minister said he was glad Elvis Presley would never
> grace another stage. My brother Vernon probably
> thought he would receive comfort from one of the
> televised ministries. Now let me set the scene for you.
> Vernon had just lost his child and you can see that
> preacher did not lift up a broken father who was sit-
> ting there with his heart so burdened. I'll tell you what
> that minister did do. He magnified the pain and the
> hurt for my brother.*
>
> *One television evangelist sent out a letter after*

Elvis passed away saying "Elvis Presley did not go to Heaven." (I don't know how I got on his mailing list, but one of those letters came to my house.) His letter continued, saying that if Elvis ever had gotten saved, he would have given up performing in the night clubs in Las Vegas.

Another television evangelist looked straight into the television camera one night on his nationwide television program and said, "Elvis Presley was a junkie, a drug addict."

Slowly, painfully, Elvis' family began to put their lives back together. They found they could laugh again. Perhaps it was because they began to get the feeling that maybe Elvis hadn't left Graceland after all. There already had been "family talk" about Graceland's ghosts.

"One night, before Elvis' death, I was staying at Graceland with Grandma," Donna explains. "It was just the two of us there. The doorbell rang. We knew it was one of the maids, so Grandma asked me if I would go let her in.

"As I went to the door, I heard footsteps behind me. I looked around and no one was there. I opened the door for the maid and then I went running back up to Grandma's room. I told her about it and she said, 'That's just Gladys (Elvis' mother). She walks around this house all the time.' "

After Elvis died, Buddy remembers one night when he was in the guard shack at the Meditation Garden at Graceland. "All of the horses came running by and then there was complete silence. It made the hair on the back of my neck stand up," he says.

Another time, Buddy was at the guard shack when the motion detector alarm inside the mansion went off. He rushed to the house, where he was met by one of the maids. "It's downstairs," she told him.

Dutifully, Buddy searched the basement, but found nothing. There was no one there, nothing had fallen that might set off the alarm. He went back upstairs and told the maid he couldn't find anything amiss, to call him if she needed him. "Then it's just Mr. P," the maid told him. "He's here all the time. Don't worry about it."

Susie also said she sometimes had the feeling she really wasn't by herself at Graceland, even when she couldn't see anybody else around. "At Graceland, you always could feel a presence," Susie says. "I don't know if it was a ghost or if Elvis just spent so much time there that you continued to feel his presence."

Once Susie was in the TV room, "all of a sudden, I felt this tug on my arm. I spun around because I thought it was one of the guards. No one was there. So I said, 'Okay, Susie, reality check here.' I turned and went into the pool room. The same thing happened.

"I high-tailed it out of there and went to the Jungle Room. The same thing happened. Finally, I just said, 'Okay, Elvis, do you want to tell me something?' That ended it. I didn't feel another tug."

Another time, when Susie was walking down the stairs directly below Elvis' bedroom, she heard footsteps overhead. "It didn't bother me because I thought it was one of the staff members going up there," she says. "But when I went up to check, no one was there."

Some staff members told Susie they heard music upstairs when no one was there. "Elvis' presence was very strong at Graceland and I think it always will be," she says.

While many things at Graceland had changed, some things still remained the same. Elvis' family still was a big part of the Graceland workforce. At one point, Nash sold tour tickets and Donna worked in Vernon's office. She remembers the day she got that job:

"It was January 3, 1979. Patsy called me up and said, 'Get up here, Uncle Vernon wants to talk to you.' So I got dressed and went up there. I walked in the office and said, 'Uncle Vernon, did you want to see me?' He looked up at me and he said, 'I thought **you** wanted to see **me**.' Then he said, 'You do want to work here, don't you?' I said, 'Yes, sir.' and he said, 'Start Monday morning.' That was one of the shortest job interviews on record. Then he said, 'We have one rule here. That is, whatever you see, whatever you hear in this office is to be kept in this office.' But that didn't surprise me. That was the way we had been raised."

The next Monday morning, Donna started answering the fan mail that continued to pour into Graceland.

Of course, Elvis' fans also continued to come to the front gate at Graceland. They simply wanted to be close to a place where he had been. It was comforting for them and it helped them keep their connection with Elvis alive.

One of the fans who came by often was a second generation Elvis fan. His mother had recounted for him many times her memories of the day she met Elvis. Sue Gray told her son:

"I think it was the spring of 1954. I was 15 years old at the time. I played piano for a trio from Marianna, Arkansas. This show was at a small community high school gym in a town just west of Marianna.

"We kept our distance from the stranger from Memphis. He was very polite, but so different. He brought a wooden folding chair and set it up where he could use it when he wasn't performing.

"We walked in and I sat down in the chair, not knowing it was his. When he finished performing, he backed up and sat down in my lap! It scared me and I stood up with a little yell.

"He apologized and said, 'I'm sorry, but that's my chair.' I said, 'Well, I didn't see your name on it.'

"We did several shows with Elvis after that and came to know him as the truly nice person that he was."

Sue's son, Buddy Early, had been raised on his mother's Elvis stories, and by the time he was 16, he was a big fan of the singer as well. "Like most teenagers, I liked fast cars, girls and football. And I had a tremendous love for music, especially Elvis'. I had almost all of his records and tapes," he says. "I can remember many nights riding around West Memphis, Arkansas — where I lived — with my friends, all of whom were Elvis fans, too. We would ride for hours, listening to his music and, of course, we sang along. I'm sure that if anyone heard us, we wouldn't have been offered a recording contract. But we thought we were good."

Then he started making trips to Memphis and driving by Graceland, "just to see where Elvis lived." Often, that's what Buddy did when he had a date. He would take the girl and they would drive by Graceland.

"I'm sure that sometimes it wasn't very exciting for her, but I loved to go by there," he says. "One night, I was driving by with a date and I finally got up enough courage to stop. My date asked what I was doing and I said, 'Let's walk up to the gate.' She said they would just run us off and I told her that they would just have to run us off then. We went over to the gate. There was no one else standing around and this older gentleman noticed me looking up at the mansion and walked out of the guard shack.

"He said he was Fred Stowe, a guard at the mansion, and I introduced myself and my date. He asked me if I would like to come into the guard shack. I felt as if I had been invited into the White House.

"We walked in and started talking to Mr. Stowe about Elvis. He asked me if I knew how to play cards and I said, 'Not much, but I'm willing to learn.' He taught me how to play Spades that night. My date got to sit in the guard shack at Graceland and watch me play cards with Mr. Stowe for hours that night."

The young man became a regular at the Graceland guard shack. He and Mr. Stowe spent many hours playing cards there. Inevitably, he began to meet the people who were allowed in and out of the gates at the mansion. One person he met was Jesse Pritchett, Nash's son, who lived behind the mansion with his mother and father.

"I thought that was so cool. Jesse was Elvis' first cousin," he says. "Since I was only a teenager, I knew all the Memphis 'hot spots.' Jesse was divorced and we started going to these places together. We became pretty good friends." Jesse and his new pal Buddy started spending a lot of time together.

"After a while, I was trusted to drive my car into the

gates at Graceland and up to Mr. and Mrs. Pritchett's mobile home," Buddy continues. "I really thought I was something. One night, Jesse and I were at a disco in Memphis and I overheard him talking about his sister. He said she was in the process of getting a divorce.

"I really started listening closely because I had met Donna and I thought she was the most beautiful woman I ever laid eyes on. But I never had gotten the courage to ask her out. One day after that, though, I was in the office behind Graceland. I don't remember why I was there, probably doing some odd job for someone.

"Donna and her cousin Patsy both were secretaries at Graceland at this time and they were in the office. I remember this day as if it were yesterday — just as I remember clearly most of the times I've been terrified. I was leaving the office, not wanting to wear out my welcome, when Donna walked over to me and said, 'Well, when are you going to ask me out?'

"There haven't been many times in my life when I was speechless, but this was one of them. Finally, I said something like, 'Sure, what about this weekend?' I can't describe how I was feeling when I left that office. I was extremely excited about going out with Donna, but I also was scared to death."

Buddy thought he was scared then, but he still had the toughest inspection to go through. He had to meet — and meet the approval of — Minnie.

"I remember the first time I met Dodger. Donna walked me in the back way at Graceland and introduced me to her grandmother," he recalls. "I remember she had a handkerchief in her hand, holding it in front of her mouth. She pulled it away and looked at me and said to Donna, 'He's a cute little thing.' Then she told me, 'But if you ever hurt my Donnie, I'll whip your little ass' and started laughing. She really was great. I guess that was one of the reasons Elvis and Donna were so crazy about her. In the short time I knew her, I felt that way, too."

A few months later, Buddy and Donna were married. If

he was going to be a part of the family, it only made sense that he also be a Graceland employee.

"I was working at a car dealership in Memphis, writing service. One day, the phone rang at my work station," he says. "There were a bunch of the other guys around. I answered it and the voice on the other end said, 'This is Vernon Presley.' I turned to the other guys and said, 'I have to have this conversation in private.' Vernon asked me if I would like to work at Graceland. He said he had heard from Donna that I was interested in a job. I told him I was interested and he asked me when I could come by for an interview. I said, 'Will this afternoon be soon enough?' I went up to Graceland and talked to Vernon. I remember he looked so sick and you couldn't help but feel the hurt that showed in his face. He told me that there soon would be an opening for a guard and that he would keep me in mind. I thanked him and then we sat in the back yard and talked for some time.

"I'll never forget that conversation. Although we had spoken on several occasions before, this was the first time he really just opened up and talked with me. I saw a side of Vernon Presley that I only can describe as genuine. He was a wonderful man, full of love, wit, wisdom and understanding."

Vernon also was a businessman who had a very good grasp on who Elvis Presley was and how he affected people. Vernon had told reporters after Elvis' death that he feared security might be a problem at the Forest Hill mausoleum. If using the cemetery's mausoleum did become a problem for the family or for the cemetery, he said, he would consider building a Presley family mausoleum. It did become a problem. So big a problem in fact, that Vernon gave up all hope of leaving Elvis and his mother buried in a public cemetery.

On August 29, only a few days after Elvis was buried, three men, armed with guns and grenades, went to the cemetery and tried to steal Elvis' body. It was reported that the men were paid more than $100,000 to steal the body and deliver it to the man who hired them. That man then planned to hold the body for a multi-million dollar ransom. They refused to identify the man who paid them. The men didn't get away with their plan to steal the body and they were arrested for trespassing.

The charges eventually were dropped because the court accepted their defense. They told the judge that it was their plan not to steal the body, but to prove that the coffin was empty and that Elvis' funeral had been a hoax. Vernon knew then that something had to be done. He could see that this was just the beginning of attempts to steal Elvis' body or prove he wasn't there.

Vernon went to the Board of Adjustments and requested a zoning variance that would allow him to bring Elvis' and Gladys' bodies back to Graceland for burial. He was granted a variance for burial of up to six bodies at Graceland.

During the night on October 2, Elvis and Gladys came back to Graceland. They were home.

"I remember the night they brought Elvis and his mother back to Graceland," Buddy says. "I was standing at the guard shack, talking to some friends at the gate. As the hearses pulled through the gate, I felt a sense of peace that Elvis and his mother were back home, especially after the attempt to steal Elvis' body from the mausoleum. But I also had such a sick feeling, knowing we never would see Elvis again, at least not in this world."

"It was good to have Aunt Gladys and Elvis back home," Donna adds. "I knew that it's the way they would have wanted it and they were together again."

A massive marker — featuring angels and a cross — that had been on Gladys' grave at Forest Hill was moved to the new gravesite, where it now would overlook both Gladys and her son. In the Meditation Garden at Graceland, Elvis' and Gladys' graves were covered with bronze markers. Vernon knew the markers should have some sort of tributes to them, but he wasn't sure what they should say.

He spent a lot of time thinking about what the markers should say. It worried him enough to keep him up at night. Finally, he decided he had to stop worrying about it for a while. When the time was right, the words would come to him. When he woke up the next morning, he knew exactly what should be on the markers.

For Elvis' marker, he wrote:

Elvis Aaron Presley

January 8, 1935
August 16, 1977

Son of Vernon Elvis Presley
and Gladys Love Presley

Father of Lisa Marie Presley

He was a precious gift from God
We cherished and loved dearly.
He had a God-given talent that
he shared with the world.
And without a doubt,
He became the most widely acclaimed;
capturing the hearts of young and old alike.
He was admired not only as an entertainer
But as the great humanitarian that he was;
For his generosity, and his kind feelings
For his fellow man.
He revolutionized the field of music and
Received its highest awards.
He became a living legend in his own time,
Earning the respect and love of millions.
God saw that he needed some rest and
Called him home to be with Him.
We miss you, Son and Daddy.
I thank God that he gave us you as our son.

By: Vernon Presley

Vernon decided Gladys' marker should say:

Gladys Love Smith Presley

April 25, 1912
August 14, 1958

Wife of Vernon Presley

Mother of Elvis Aaron Presley
and
Jessie Garon Presley

She was a great person, a great wife and mother.
She was also loved by many.
We loved her dearly and she is sadly missed.

By: Vernon Presley

Though Elvis' twin isn't buried at Graceland, a memorial to him was placed in the Meditation Garden as well.

Vernon was as much aware of his son's fans as Elvis was. He knew they wanted to visit Elvis' grave. Now that he had it secured at Graceland, he could make that possible. On November 27, the Meditation Garden area of Graceland's grounds was opened to the public. Visitors could walk up the drive and visit Elvis' final resting place.

Set in a small courtyard with red tile walkways, large white columns and a pool with six fountains, the gravesite was open from 9 a.m. to 4 p.m. Tuesday through Sundays.

Naturally, more access to Graceland meant more security. Buddy became a guard at the gravesite.

"After the gravesite opened, I found that Monday, the day we were closed to the public, was my longest day. I worked 12 hours on Mondays, but I had plenty to keep me busy," he says. "I cleaned the pool out and kept the gravesites clean. I put fresh flowers on the gravesite daily. That wasn't hard because every day, arrangements arrived, sent from people all over the globe.

"I met a lot of really great people up at that gravesite who were just like I was — in awe of a man who had a God-given talent, who we all respected more than you can imagine."

Just as they had before Elvis' death, the fans added a touch of excitement to the atmosphere at Graceland after he died.

Buddy remembers one night when he was watching the front gate:

"More than a year after Elvis' death, a lady came up with a baby and said, 'Is Elvis here?' "

As politely as he knew how, Buddy told her Elvis wasn't at Graceland. "She said she knew he was and that she demanded to see him. 'I'm his wife,' she said. 'This is his baby.' I said, 'Elvis is dead. He's buried on the grounds here.'

"She said, 'He's not dead, I saw him the other day.' "

Realizing that there was no reasoning with the woman, Buddy turned and walked away.

"One of the other guards called and said, 'Buddy you might want to come back out here.' I go back out and the woman has left the baby laying right where the gates come together. It's 12:30 or 1 a.m. and we have to call the Memphis Police and Child Protective Services to get the baby. I don't know what happened to that baby, but I would like to."

That woman wasn't the only person to claim some kind of legal connection with Elvis. Once Donna was at the gravesite when a woman came up to her and said, "Is Elvis here?"

"I said something like, 'Only in the fact that he's buried here,' " Donna says. "Then she says, 'I need to see his father.' "

When Donna asked why, the woman said, "His father is my father."

"I said 'I don't think so' or something like that," Donna says. "Then she said, 'Is Earl Pritchett here?' That's when it really started getting strange. I asked her why she needed to know that and she said, 'He's my grandfather.' I told her

Earl was my father and I was sure she was mistaken."

Another fan's devotion touched Buddy deeply:

"There was this girl from New Zealand — her first name was Kathy," he says. "She had worked at a hamburger joint and saved for two years to come to Memphis. She got there about six months after Elvis died. She stayed for a year and she came to the gravesite every single day. She brought a rose and she would just sit there, away from everybody else for a while, then leave."

Eventually, Graceland was made even more accessible to Elvis' fans. With mixed emotions on everyone's part, the decision was made that the house and grounds would have to be opened for tours. It wasn't opened until after Vernon's death, but he had talked often about the fact that it probably would be open this way some day. Nash remembered:

> *Graceland opened to the public June 7, 1982. We all knew something had to be done to bring in revenue. I don't think most people realize the money it takes to operate a place as large as Graceland. Vernon had talked about it many times. He had thought about creating a back entrance for visitors that would bring them up by the Meditation Garden and the trophy room. He thought about building a crosswalk from the property across the street and letting the people come onto the grounds that way. I think Vernon wanted to do what would be the best thing for Lisa Marie in the long run.*

Though they saw the logic and practicality of opening Graceland for tours, having what had been their home opened to the public wasn't an easy adjustment for Elvis' family. "At first I thought of it as an invasion of privacy — people coming through Elvis' home," Susie says. "But then, Elvis was proud of his house, so he always had people there."

Another thing family members found themselves having to get used to was the fact that they no longer could go anywhere on the hill any time they wanted. "Once after they opened the home to the public, I was walking across the lawn and someone says to me, 'Keep off the grass,' " Donna remembers. "I had a hard time not telling them that I had been walking on that grass practically ever since I could walk."

Naturally, if there were to be tours of Graceland, there would have to be tickets for the tours. Nash sold those tickets to the public for a number of years. Most of the time, the fans who bought their tickets from her didn't know they were buying them from one of Elvis' most beloved relatives.

And, if there were to be tours, there would have to be tour guides. Once again, the Presley family looked among themselves for employees. Susie became a tour guide, taking people through her home. "At first, it was difficult, the memories were immediate," she says. She didn't tell people who she was, but many of them sensed that she had a special passion for the home and asked her why. Then she told them, "I'm Elvis' cousin. This is my home."

Susie found that, for the most part, she enjoyed taking the fans through Graceland. They seemed to be grateful to his family for sharing this personal part of their lives and they had nice things to say about Elvis. She learned to ignore the people touring Graceland who didn't have nice things to say about the singer and his family.

And she learned to control her laughter when the people taking the tour caught her off guard. At the time, she explains, instead of taking a self-guided audio tour the way visitors do today, a guide took each group through a part of the mansion.

"One day, I was standing in the dining room, getting ready for the next group of people coming through. I was looking at the table and the chandelier. Just another day at Graceland. Then I look up as the group walked in and here was this man dressed like Snow White — gown, wig and all. The man with him was dressed like Elvis. Somehow, I managed to compose myself and get through the speech. I don't know how. I mean it's not like you see something like that every day.

"Another time, I was working in the living room/music room. Because this room is large, the speech here is longer than most. I was standing there ready to start and I notice this middle-aged man in the front of the group. He was wearing a baseball cap with the brim turned up and the hem of his pants hit him about mid-calf. He was wearing huge white sunglasses. He's just standing there, grinning at me like a possum. I started my speech the same way I always did by saying, 'Please step all the way up to the ropes so everyone can get in.' And he pulls his pants up even higher. Now his belt is at his underarms. That was one day when I had to give my speech without looking at the group because every time I did, I broke up."

Another spot in the mansion that Susie remembers well is the staircase that goes to the basement. Surrounding it are mirrors arranged so that anyone looking in them sees many, many reflections of himself. Often, Susie heard people going down the steps say, "Boy, Elvis must have loved to look at himself."

"On this particular day, though, this large woman had just made that comment, looking at herself the whole time," Susie remembers, "Suddenly she was hurtling down the stairs head first. A security guard and a tour guide were standing at the bottom of the stairs and they scattered like leaves in the wind."

A teenage boy once provided the humor on one of Susie's tours. This time, she was in the Jungle Room:

"This teenager was going through with his parents. He had a real attitude. In the place where the group stood to hear about the Jungle Room, there is a wall that's covered with fabric. You can't see it, but there's a door behind the fabric. Well, the boy's standing there with his arms crossed, trying to look super cool. Then he leaned back against the wall. One minute, he was there. The next minute, he wasn't. The door must not have been closed well because it had opened and he had fallen backwards right through it. That was the end of his attitude."

Another time, Delta met the fans quite by accident. "I

Earl Pritchett
702 Dover
West Memphis, AR. 72301

Dear Earl,

On Tuesday, June 7th, we marked the one year anniversary of the opening of Graceland to the public. I want to take this opportunity to personally thank you for all that you have done to make this first year such a great success.

Your hard work and sincere efforts have helped to create Graceland's international reputation. I have received reports from around the world that we have the finest and most caring people working for us.

I know that Elvis would be extremely proud of the way you have contributed in helping to keep the integrity and the historical importance of Graceland.

Thank you from the bottom of my heart for making my wish become a reality.

Sincerely,

Priscilla Presley

Earl. You've done a fine job keeping things together around Graceland keep up the good work it is noticed.

Letters from Priscilla Presley in 1983 to Nash and Earl Pritchett, expressing her appreciation for their service at Graceland.

Earl Pritchett
702 Dover
West Memphis, AR. 72301

Dear Earl,

On Tuesday, June 7th, we marked the one year anniversary of the opening of Graceland to the public. I want to take this opportunity to personally thank you for all that you have done to make this first year such a great success.

Your hard work and sincere efforts have helped to create Graceland's international reputation. I have received reports from around the world that we have the finest and most caring people working for us.

I know that Elvis would be extremely proud of the way you have contributed in helping to keep the integrity and the historical importance of Graceland.

Thank you from the bottom of my heart for making my wish become a reality.

Sincerely,

Priscilla Presley

Earl. You've done a fine job keeping things together around Graceland keep up the good work it is noticed.

was coming up behind the group," Susie explains, "and I didn't know the tour guide before me had left the ropes down and everyone had just filed into the part of the kitchen area where Aunt Delta stayed. About the time I got there, Aunt Delta was in the middle of the group and she was saying, 'How the hell did you get in here?' The people in the group were as surprised as Aunt Delta."

Susie wasn't easily fooled by the fans who tried to get her to bend the Graceland rules:

"At the time, the visitors went out on the carport to see Elvis' motorcycles, the pink Cadillac and his other cars and vehicles," she says. "One day, this guy came through with his wife. And I could tell he loved Elvis' Harley-Davidson. He says to me, 'You sure are pretty and you sure have gorgeous eyes.' I said, 'Thank you, but you're not going to get to sit on that motorcycle and have your picture made.' That was the end of his interest in me."

Sometimes, it was the other tour guides, not the visitors, who made Susie laugh:

"There are deer horns above the door as you enter the TV room," she explains. "Now you also have to remember that there are mirrors on the ceiling in the TV room. One of the other tour guides sneaks in at the back of my group, takes down the deer horns and puts them on his head. I'm giving my speech and I look up at the mirrors. And there's this guy with the deer horns on his head. It was quite a sight."

And sometimes, it was Susie herself who provided the humor:

"In part of the trophy building, there was a place where some of Elvis' guitars were hanging from the ceiling," she says. "I threw my hand up to point at them. I hit one of them and it swung and hit me in the head. I tried to move over a little and it swung back the other way and hit me on the other side of the head. That was one day when I really heard the music."

In another part of the building is the tuxedo Elvis wore when he accepted the "Outstanding Young Man" award. It was displayed on a mannequin. "Well, I also was one to gesture a lot," Susie says. "So we're there by the tuxedo and I gesture toward it and all of a sudden, it just disappears. I had hit the mannequin and knocked it over."

Another time when Susie was directing a tour in that part of the building, she was standing by the tuxedo and giving her speech, but she noticed that her audience seemed to be looking around for something and they appeared to be very confused. "Finally, another tour guide came up and said, 'Susie, you're giving the speech for the Jungle Room. You've got them looking for the waterfall.' The people at Graceland said I was one of the best guides they had. I'm glad they didn't see me on that day."

Since Graceland opened to the public, millions of people have taken the tour and it remains one of Tennessee's and the nation's top tourist spots. The numbers don't surprise Buddy. As soon as the mansion opened to the public, he realized the kind of following Elvis had.

"I was amazed at the impact this man had on the world — people of all ages and races from every country around the globe. I met people from other countries who had saved for years just to come to Graceland," he says. "I met people who left well-paying jobs where they had worked for decades to come to Memphis and get jobs working at souvenir shops near Graceland, just to be near where Elvis was. I met people who had had cosmetic surgery so they would look more like Elvis. I met people who had named their children after him."

15

"The SOBs that did it are walking around."

ELVIS HAD BEEN DEAD a little more than a year when Donna went to work at Graceland. Her job was to work in Vernon's office with Patsy (Vester's daughter). Together, she and Patsy would open and answer the fan mail that came in. It may seem odd to some people that fan mail would continue to pour into Graceland so long after Elvis' death, but Donna and Patsy understood. "When Elvis died, his fans just transferred what they felt for him to us — the members of his family," Donna says.

"The people who wrote those letters identified with Elvis and his family," she remembers. "I can't tell you how many times I opened letters that said, 'I lost my mother when I was very young and Elvis' music comforted me so much' or 'I was abused when I was a child and the only time I was truly happy was when I was in my room, listening to my Elvis records.' That was just what Elvis did for people. It was incredible to think about the ways that he helped so many people."

Before taking this job, Donna had not gotten to know Vernon very well. He was a handsome man who wore his gruff exterior like a suit of armor protecting him from the feelings that would cause displays of emotion. Men weren't

275

necessarily "in touch with their feminine sides" at this point in American history and they didn't cry in public or show affection with sons and brothers if they could help it. Spending day after day at work together began to make Vernon's armor wear thin where Donna was concerned. She began to look at him as a wise counselor ("There wasn't anything I couldn't ask him about.") and he began to recognize her for the intelligent, lovely woman she was. They became fast friends.

Which probably is why Vernon felt he could tell Donna what he did one day in mid-1979. Patsy had left for the day, so Donna and Vernon were alone in the office. "We were sitting there and we'd work a little bit and we'd talk a little bit. Then he leaned back in his chair and put his feet up on his desk and he just sighed really big, like he had the weight of the world on his shoulders," Donna remembers. "I asked him, 'Uncle Vernon, what's wrong? Is there something I can help you with? Something I can do for you?' "

Vernon turned and looked away from Donna and out the window toward the Meditation Garden and Elvis' grave. Then he spoke again. "He said, 'You know I can't stand it that my baby's in the ground out there and those others are still walking around.' I thought he was just making a general statement on the condition of the world, how good people sometimes die and people who seem so evil are still alive, so I said, 'Yes, Uncle Vernon, it is a shame.' Then he said, 'You don't understand what I mean. It just kills me that my baby's laying out there in that cold ground and the SOBs that did it are walking around.' I said, 'What do you mean?'"

Vernon looked at Donna and said, "The people who killed Elvis." Since the idea that Elvis might have died anything other than a natural death had never occurred to Donna, she was caught off-guard. "I said, 'What are you talking about, Uncle Vernon?' And he said, 'Elvis was murdered.' I couldn't believe what I was hearing. I thought he meant that there was just so much responsibility on Elvis and that's what ended up killing him. I said, 'Exactly what do you mean he was murdered?' He looked right at me and said, 'Exactly what I said. Somebody murdered him.' "

Donna suddenly realized her heart was racing as she tried to figure out how best to help Vernon. "I said, 'Uncle Vernon, do you have proof?' He said, 'Yes, I do. I've got proof.' " Donna felt a chill as Vernon began to explain what he thought happened to his son. Vernon said — and *The Death of Elvis: What Really Happened* seems to bear this out — that even Dr. Nichopoulos had become worried about how many drugs Elvis was taking. Not wanting to alarm his patient, he simply began substituting placebos for the real thing from time to time, thus lowering Elvis' dosages without his realizing it. However, the day he died, Vernon said, Elvis had gotten a full dose of all the medicines, enough to cause him to show the symptoms of an overdose of drugs.

By this time, Donna's hand was on the phone. "I said, 'We should call the police. We need to tell them about it.' " Vernon's look stopped Donna from even lifting the receiver. "He said, 'No, I'm not telling the police. I don't want anybody else to know about this. This is a family matter. I will take care of it. I will get them myself in my own way.' I said, 'Uncle Vernon, what are you talking about? What do you mean you'll get them?' He said, 'Just that, I'll get them in my own way. Elvis wouldn't want this to be known. He would just have wanted it to be taken care of.' "

Donna had to respect Vernon's wishes. After all, he was the one with the evidence and he was right about what Elvis would have wanted. "Elvis always said he didn't want anybody getting famous off the fact that he was the one who killed Elvis Presley. When people had threatened his life, he had told the guys, 'If he gets me, you get him. I don't want anybody getting famous because he was the person who killed Elvis Presley.' "

Donna wasn't going to take what she had heard off the hill, but she couldn't keep it to herself — it bothered her too much. That evening, she headed for Nash's trailer and a talk with her mother. "I told her what Uncle Vernon had said and she seemed to know about it already. I said, 'Mom, we need to tell somebody.' And she said, 'No, we don't. Just keep quiet and let Vernon handle it.' So I did."

Just a few months later, Vernon was dead. His revelation, his evidence, his plans for revenge all were buried with him. Donna said her good-byes to the man she had come to respect so much, but she couldn't get that conversation off her mind. Once again, she approached Nash about it. Donna remembers her mother's answer: "I don't want you to say anything because what you can tell you have no proof of and we don't know where it is. Saying something about it isn't going to bring Elvis back." But in the next breath, Nash revealed the real reason she wanted Donna to keep what Vernon had told her a secret: "They've killed Elvis and you could be next. This could end up getting you killed. You've got two little boys to take care of and, without proof, telling it isn't going to change a thing."

That day, Donna promised Nash she never would reveal what Vernon had told her in the office. Now that Nash has died and Donna's children are grown, she feels it's time to talk about what Vernon said.

"It's time that it was told. I want everyone to know that Uncle Vernon believed Elvis was murdered, no doubt about it. And I believe Uncle Vernon," she says. "And now whoever did it will realize they didn't get away with it at all.

"I guess they got away with it in the legal sense. They'll never be arrested for it and they won't ever be judged here on earth, but they eventually will be judged for what they did — and by a higher judge than they ever would face here. I feel that it's something that needs to be said. I don't know how they get up and look at themselves in the mirror every morning knowing what they did to someone who trusted them and cared about them as much as Elvis did."

Some time later, Nash told Edie about the things Donna had shared with her that day. "It was at a time when people really were starting to write books about Elvis and she wanted me to be careful who I talked to or who I worked with," Edie says. "She called me to come to Arkansas so she could tell me face to face.

"On the day Donna told her, Nash had called me and

asked me to pray about a problem Donna was having, but she said she didn't want to tell me what the problem was. She told me I needed to pray that the Lord would protect Donna. I could understand it all when she told me what Vernon had told Donna."

Sometimes, Donna says, she wishes Vernon hadn't shared his suspicions with her. "It changed the way I felt about people I thought were friends," she says, "and for that reason, I wish I didn't know."

After Vernon told Donna about how he thought Elvis had died, she began to understand the depth of Vernon's grief for his son. They were everything to one another, did everything for one another. To lose Elvis would be hard enough, to know that someone took him away was almost more than Vernon could bear.

"I know Vernon did have a bad heart," Nash wrote in her memoirs, "but I always will believe he died of a broken heart."

Donna's husband Buddy agrees. "After Elvis died," he recalls, "every afternoon, he would go to his house and play Elvis' gospel records over and over. You could hear it carrying all over the hill. Vernon grieved himself to death."

To add to the pain of losing his son, Vernon also had received a copy of the autopsy performed on Elvis. There were only a few people besides Vernon who knew what that document said, but something about it haunted Elvis' father for the rest of his life. Donna would discover why when she decided to come forward about Elvis' death.

If Vernon received the same information that the authors of "the autopsy book" did, he probably learned that Elvis' lungs looked okay, that his heart was slightly larger than normal and that his brain looked normal. He would have found that Elvis didn't die from a pulmonary embolism, an aneurysm, a heart attack or a stroke. What Cole and Thompson say in their book is that, on the night Elvis died, the doctors had not yet performed enough tests to determine why Elvis died. They ruled out all the obvious things and were going to have to look deeper to find the cause. Tissue and blood tests would have to hold the answers if the answers were going to come.

So why did doctors report at the news conference that night that Elvis had died of a heart attack? That's a mystery to many of the people involved, according to Thompson and Cole. Apparently, the doctors who stayed behind working on further autopsy results had thought that the official word given at the press conference would be that they needed more time to discover the cause of death. Some of those people told Thompson and Cole that they were as surprised as everyone else when the heart attack diagnosis was announced that night.

Because of that confusion and simply the fact that Elvis Presley was involved, there were plenty of rumors floating around about why Elvis died. "I knew that Vernon was suspicious about the cause of Elvis' death," Thompson says. In the process of writing his book, Thompson encountered other people with whom Vernon had discussed his thoughts about Elvis' death.

Vernon wanted answers and he was willing to wait until he had the full autopsy report before he came to any conclusions. When he did get that report, it seems that the worst scenario he could have imagined was the only one that made sense.

"I haven't read a lot of the books that have been written about Elvis," Donna says. "The reasons should be obvious. And I haven't read 'the autopsy book,' but once we decided to do this book, I've read enough to know that Uncle Vernon could have been right."

According to the book, tests showed that there were a number of drugs at or above toxic levels in Elvis' blood. There were others that were near toxic levels. Vernon probably had found this out when he was given a copy of the autopsy results.

And, the book reveals, there was one other thing in the report that might have concerned Vernon. Elvis, according to some of his friends, was allergic to codeine. He had been given a prescription for it once and, when he took it, he began to swell, get short of breath and itch, classic early signs of an anaphylactic reaction. And when Elvis' body was discovered in the bathroom at Graceland, there were signs that he may have suffered such a reaction again. His tongue was swollen so badly that he had bitten through it. He had vomited on the carpet.

The autopsy report, which Vernon had seen, also showed the presence of codeine in Elvis' bloodstream. Why would a man who knew he was allergic to codeine take it? Perhaps because one tablet form of codeine looks very much like the tablet form of the Dilaudid® that Elvis regularly took for pain. While Thompson and Cole conclude that Elvis died of an accidental overdose of drugs, Vernon had a different take on it altogether. Somewhere, somehow, it seemed to Vernon that perhaps one drug deliberately had been substituted for the other by someone other than Elvis. And Elvis had died as a result.

Of course, Donna has thought over the years about why anyone would want to murder Elvis. In today's world, people murder people every day for all sorts of reasons. Often, though, the motives seem to have a common theme — money or jealousy or fear.

Since Vernon never told her all the things he learned about Elvis' death, Donna has been left to speculate what a motive might be. "Perhaps someone thought Elvis wasn't making the right business decisions. Perhaps one person thought another was getting more from Elvis than he was. Or maybe someone feared he was about to fall from Elvis' good graces. Or maybe drugs played a part," she says.

Donna, like members of many other victims' families, has found that motivation for violence is difficult to understand. "In the mind of someone who loved the victim, there is no motivation strong enough to justify taking that life," Donna explains.

This many years removed from Elvis' death, Donna says she has come to wonder less about why her cousin would have been murdered. After all, knowing a motive wouldn't change the one thing that matters most to her — that Elvis is dead.

Through reading parts of Thompson and Cole's book, Donna has learned one thing that makes knowing about Elvis' death even worse. Elvis didn't die instantly. "And that seems to support what Uncle Vernon told me about Elvis' murder. I think that's one thing that probably bothered Uncle Vernon a lot. Someone could have helped Elvis and no one did.

"It really makes me sad to think about it. I worry that he might have been conscious for a while. I try to imagine what he must have thought. At first, I think, he probably assumed somebody would come to help him and then realized that they weren't coming. If he did, he must have figured out what was going on. I know that it would have hurt him to think about being betrayed like that. And I'm sure that if he lay there conscious for any time, he would have thought about his mother. And I'm sure he would have thought about Uncle Vernon and Grandma, too, worrying about who would take care of them.

"Elvis might not have lived the perfect life, but he never gave up that religion that was so much a part of his upbringing, so I'm sure he would have spent some time getting right with the Lord.

"And I know he would have thought about Lisa Marie. I know he would have been concerned about this happening while she was at Graceland. He never would have wanted it to be that way. He would have worried about who would take care of her until Priscilla got there to be with her. In the end, I know he would have just put them all in the Lord's hands so he could have some peace. It really saddens me to think he must have died that way. I can't imagine how much it must have hurt Uncle Vernon."

Donna realizes that she will take some criticism for talking about Elvis' murder so long after it happened. People, she knows, probably will doubt her motives — thinking she's done this to capitalize on Elvis' name. But she dismisses those people. "They will just have to think that. I have to tell this now," she explains. "Now others will at least know what Uncle Vernon believed happened."

16

"Always ... in my heart and mind."

WHEN VERNON PRESLEY WALKED up to his son's coffin at Graceland, he told Elvis that he would be with him soon. His words echoed in the ears of his family in mid-1979 as Vernon's health began to decline. Elvis' father had suffered a heart attack in 1975, so his family knew he was vulnerable to cardiac problems.

One day in June, 1979, Vernon told Vester that he had felt faint as he walked between his office and Graceland. About 4 p.m., the fire department near Graceland got a call to the well-known address once again. Someone there, they were told, was having chest pain. The rescue unit arrived and worked with Vernon for about 30 minutes, then left Graceland headed for Baptist Hospital. Twenty-two months earlier, the patient on board had been Elvis. On this day, it was his father. Vernon was admitted to the hospital's Intensive Care Unit. By 5 p.m., his condition had been stabilized, but he still was a seriously ill man.

His fiancee and nurse, Sandy Miller, had ridden to the hospital in the ambulance with him. She took up her post by his bedside and was joined there by his sisters Delta and Nash.

"When Uncle Vernon was sick in his last days, Mom and

Delta went to the hospital to see him every day," Donna says. "They made sure he had anything and everything he needed. Sandy stayed there with him all the time. Mom and Delta would go back and forth to the house so they could bring him anything he wanted. Of course, they also went to the hospital just to be with him. They all were very, very close."

Nash became such a fixture in the Intensive Care Unit that one of Vernon's doctors began calling her "Sis." As Nash recalled:

> That's what Delta called me and I guess he just picked it up from her. That doctor told me that when he started treating Vernon, he thought he would teach Vernon a lot of things, but "that man taught me so much instead." I know there were times when I irritated the doctor because he would tell me something they were going to try on Vernon and he would say, "If this doesn't work, he's gone." I would say, "No, he's going to make it." And he would say, "Sis, there's nothing to build on."
>
> I remember one time we were in the hall outside the ICU and they were going to put a pacemaker on Vernon and the doctor said, "If this doesn't work, we may lose him." I told him I knew what he was saying, clinically speaking, but I knew God was going to take care of Vernon. I showed him in the Bible some scripture to back up what I was saying. Several times after that, it looked like Vernon was not going to make it but he, by the grace of God, did make it.

When Sandy would take a break and come to Graceland to change clothes or get something she needed, she sometimes would stop by to talk to Donna and Patsy. "She'd say, 'He is so sick and he's so weak and he's suffered so much. Why doesn't God just take him?' I was shocked," Donna says. "I thought, 'My God, how cold and unfeeling can she be? She's wanting him to die.'

"Then when my mom got sick and I was with her that very last day when we took her off life support, I prayed for her to die. I thought if anybody else heard me do that, they would think how horrible I was. I understood what Sandy had meant then."

As sick as Vernon was, he still talked to his sister about his plans for when he left the hospital. Nash remembered:

> *The day before Vernon passed away, I was sitting with him and he said, "I would like to get in my car and drive down through Florida, take a leisure trip." That same day, he took two of my fingers between his fingers and told me as soon as he got out of the hospital, he would come to my church.*
>
> *The day Vernon passed away, Delta and I had gotten to the hospital, gotten off the elevator and started down the hall to his room. We saw the doctor and Sandy coming down to meet us. Sandy was crying and we knew something was wrong. When they got close to us, the doctor put his arm around us and said, "Come go with us." He took us to a room — I believe it was the chapel — and he told us that Vernon had just passed away. After the necessary calls were made, Delta and I rushed back to Graceland to tell Mom before she heard it on the news.*
>
> *Before we left the hospital, though, we told the doctor we wanted to see Vernon. So we went into his room and I put my hand on his forehead. I stood there and said a silent prayer. Our brother had slipped away from us.*
>
> *Delta, Vernon and I became very close during the time of his illness. And for that we always will be thankful.*
>
> *Fortunately, Mom had not heard about Vernon before we got back to Graceland. When we went in, the maids were in the kitchen. I told them Vernon had passed away and they started crying rather loudly. I said, "S-h-h, Mom will hear you." So they got quiet*

and I went to tell Mom. I knelt down beside her chair. She took one look at me and said, "Vernon's dead, isn't he?" I said, "Yes, Mom, they did all they could for him." Mom just had told Donna that she felt very uneasy about Vernon and she was afraid he wasn't going to live much longer.

Vernon's body was brought back to Graceland to lie in state, just the way his son's had been. Nash recalled that time:

> *Mom was quite a trooper through the time Vernon lay in state there at Graceland and during the funeral and graveside rites.*

One thing Minnie did at that time, however, disturbed Donna. "The words that Uncle Vernon had said standing next to Elvis' casket came back to me. Grandma said the same thing standing beside her son's casket. She looked at Uncle Vernon and said, 'Son, I'll be with you soon.' It's strange, but somehow I knew when she spoke those words that it wouldn't be long before she was gone."

Once again, it was time for the Presley family to gather to say good-bye to one of their own. Priscilla and Lisa Marie flew in from California and Aunt Delta dispatched Donna and Buddy to pick them up at the airport. Linda Thompson arrived. Colonel Parker got there. In a quiet, personal service, conducted by Rev. M.H. Kennedy and Rev. C.W. Bradley — who had conducted Elvis' funeral — Vernon Presley's life was celebrated and his death mourned. After the service, his family followed the coffin to the Meditation Garden. Vernon was laid to rest with Elvis and Gladys. The three of them were home again — together at Graceland.

True to the tradition Vernon had established, his family decided what they wanted his marker to say. For Vernon's, they chose:

Vernon Elvis Presley
April 10, 1916
June 26, 1979

Son of Jesse D. Presley
and
Minnie Mae Presley

Father of
Elvis Aaron Presley
and
Jessie Garon Presley

Grandfather of
Lisa Marie Presley

For when that one Great Scorer comes
To write against your name
He writes not that you won or lost
But how you played the game.

Our beloved Vernon was always a man
to look up to. He touched each of our lives with love,
protected his own and truly was the keeper of the flame.
Quietly and reverently, he carried his responsibilities in
gentle ways. He shared his wisdom and his strength,
endurance and understanding allowed him to be,
above all, a fair man to everyone.

Love is patient and endureth all things

God's finger touched him and he slept
Tennyson

Though you are gone from us, we will forever hold you
close in our hearts with precious memories.

Slowly, Vernon's family tried to get back to normal. "After Vernon's death, things at Graceland remained pretty much the same," Buddy explains. "Donna still was answering fan mail and Patsy was working in the office. Donna's dad still was working on the grounds. Aunt Delta and Dodger still were living at Graceland and Uncle Vester still was working at the front gate."

Some things about Minnie never were going to change. Her family knew and accepted that. In fact, they saw these as endearing qualities. Just as they had for Elvis, Dodger's constants brought a continuity to their lives. There were some things they always could count on.

"Grandma hated gray hair," says Donna. "She dyed her hair until the day she died."

"Every Monday, if it wasn't raining, Earl had to take Dodger's mattress and bed covers outside and sun them," Buddy adds. "It was a custom-built bed — 9 x 9 — so it was no small job. But I thought that was so cool."

Early in 1980, Minnie got a respiratory infection that seemed to overwhelm her tall, slender body. By April, she was bedridden. Delta and Nash urged their mother to let them admit her to the hospital, but Minnie saw no point in that. She never had been in a hospital, she told her daughters, and she wasn't about to go into one now.

Donna sensed that this was no ordinary illness Minnie had. She knew, in her heart of hearts, that her grandmother was near death. "My family's always been very intuitive, especially when it comes to each other," she explains.

"Grandma had been sick and I had spent as much time with her as possible," Donna says. "But I had a family of my own that needed to be taken care of. However, I did see Grandma every day even if it was for a short while.

"Buddy and I wanted to take a few days off and take his mom and stepfather to Florida for Mother's Day. His mother never had been there and we felt it would be a nice Mother's Day gift. I felt very uneasy about leaving town with Grandma being so sick. I went to see her the day we left.

"She was feeling much better. She told me to go ahead

because she was feeling better. She said she hadn't felt this good in a long time. We left and drove to Panama City, Florida. But all the way down there, I kept telling Buddy that something was wrong. I didn't know what was wrong, but I had this tremendous feeling of depression, this feeling that something was going wrong.

"When we got to the hotel, I called home immediately to let everyone know that we had arrived safely and to find out how Grandma was. My sister answered the phone. She said, 'Sis' and I guess my heart just stopped. It was the tone of her voice. Then she said, 'Grandma's gone. She died this morning.' After that, everything was a blur. I only know what happened because Buddy told me."

"I'll never forget that day," Buddy says. "I gave Donna a tranquilizer because she was so upset. I really was worried about her. We drove to Pensacola so Donna and I could catch a flight back. My mother and stepfather said they would drive my car back to Memphis.

"When we got in the air, there was a terrible storm. I thought we were going down any minute. (Later, when I told Donna about it, she asked me why I didn't wake her up during the storm. I said, 'What? You wanted me to wake you up to tell you that you were going to die?') Thank God, we landed safely in Atlanta. But the problem was we landed at Gate 2 and had less than 30 minutes to get to Gate 98 for our connecting flight to Memphis. Donna wasn't going to be any help, because she was so out of it. I knew I was going to have to carry her and our luggage through the airport.

"I can only imagine what people thought when they saw me running through the Atlanta airport carrying a semi-conscious woman and a large suitcase. But we made the flight and got back to Memphis."

Less than a year after Vernon's burial, the Presleys were back at Graceland again for another funeral. In a 1980s movie, one of the characters tells the others, "No man should ever have to bury his child." Minnie Mae Presley would have understood exactly what the man was talking about. She had buried not only a child, but a grandchild. The emotional toll had been great. She had felt it weighing heavily on her when she stood by Vernon's casket.

Minnie's family buried her at Graceland with Elvis, Vernon and Gladys. Nash wrote the inscription for her marker:

Minnie Mae Presley
June 17, 1890
May 8, 1980

Her children rise up and call her blessed;
her husband also and he praiseth her.
Proverbs 31:28

She was a gracious lady, our mother,
and a virtuous woman.
In simplicity she taught us,
With a God-given wisdom,
she guided us through hardships and
heartaches and taught us to look
to God for our strength.
She was love in motion and with
a quiet, sweet, gentle and humble spirit,
she was our close and trusted friend
and a friend to all who knew
her and she was loved by many.
A flower that never faded,
she was the queen of our home.
We love you, Mom, and we deeply miss you.

In memory of Vernon Elvis

With love,
Nash Lorene Pritchett
Delta May Biggs
Gladys Earline Dowling
Vester Lee Presley

Nash also designed the five hearts on the marker — one for each of Minnie's children. "Since Vernon had passed away, I drew the arrow from his name to ours," Nash explained.

"Now Grandma, Uncle Vernon, Aunt Gladys and Elvis all were together once again," Donna says. But Graceland, she adds, never would be the same.

Every loss the Presley family had suffered had been hard to bear, but Minnie's death may have been the hardest. "I knew I had lost the best friend I ever had apart from God the day she died," Nash said.

"I still miss Grandma so much," Donna says. "She always was there for me to talk to. She would guide me and tell me what she thought but she never was critical or condescending. I never can remember her ever saying a harsh or unkind or hurtful word to me my entire life. How many people can you say that about? She always was there for me, no matter what the situation."

"My grandmother was the most gracious lady I ever have known outside of my own mother," Susie says. "She always had a kind word for everyone. She loved people. I guess that's where Elvis got his love of people. She always was a lady, no matter what.

"She was a lady of great moral convictions. She helped teach Elvis those ways and that's what made him such a great person."

Buddy fondly remembers Minnie as "a class act."

Minnie was gone and Delta lived alone at Graceland. With Minnie's death, the Presley family members found themselves without focus, without an anchor. They always had understood intellectually that death was an inevitable part of life, but now they were learning it with their hearts. It was a hard lesson.

Slowly, the family was slipping away. Nash remembered the next death:

On December 19, 1985, our middle sister, Gladys, passed away in her sleep at her home in Tallahassee, Florida. Needless to say, it was a shock.

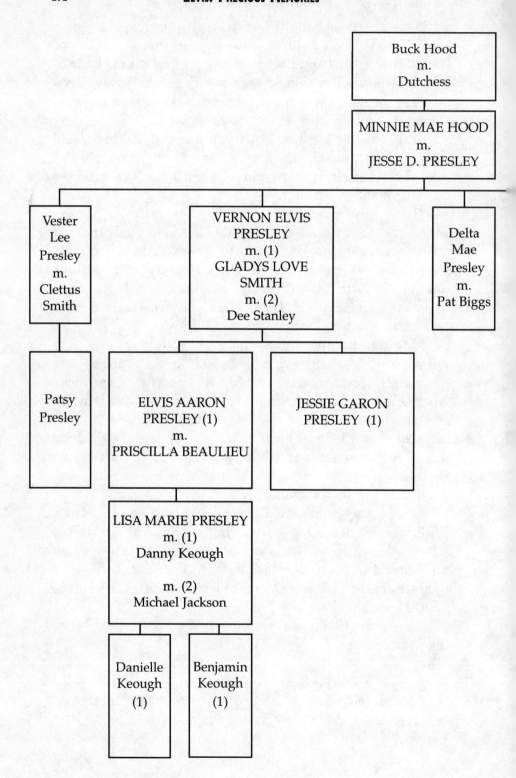

The family tree of Donna Presley Early.

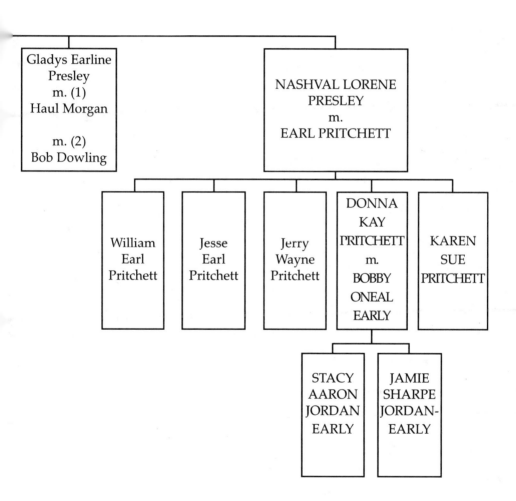

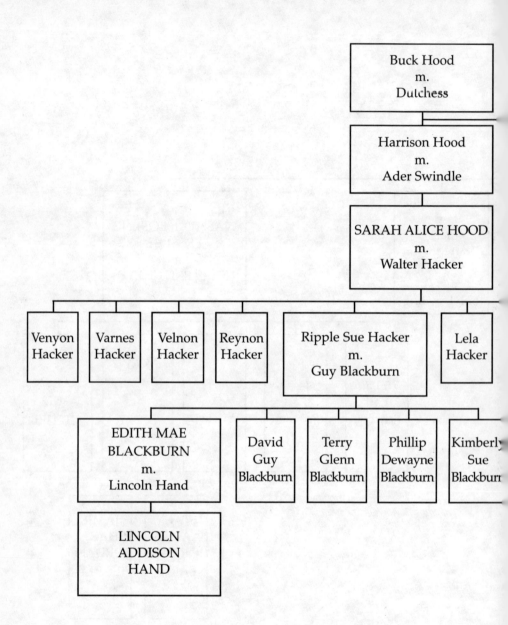

The family tree of Edie Hand.

MINNIE MAE HOOD
m.
JESSE D. PRESLEY

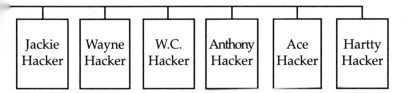

| Jackie Hacker | Wayne Hacker | W.C. Hacker | Anthony Hacker | Ace Hacker | Hartty Hacker |

Vester, Delta and I flew down there for the funeral. I preached the funeral at the request of her sons and her husband. Gladys was a precious person.

Gladys, the only one of Jesse and Minnie's children never to work at Graceland, was buried near her home in Florida.

Delta died in July, 1993, and is buried in Memphis. For the first time since Elvis bought the house, there wasn't a Presley in residence at Graceland.

Nash became ill in 1994. Over her objections, Donna took her to a specialist and she was admitted to the hospital. Nash died April 25, 1994. Her funeral was in the Wynne, Arkansas, Assembly of God Church. She is buried in a cemetery in Wynne.

"My mother quit school at the age of 15 and married my dad," Donna says. "She raised four children practically by herself because my dad had to be gone all the time. But after we were grown, my mother went back to vo-tech, got her GED and she went to Bible College, a correspondence Bible college, where she became an ordained minister in the Assembly of God. That was after all her kids were grown.

"It's never too late to strive for your goals and you're never too old to start over. She made practically a whole new life for herself as a minister. She served the community as a minister, she witnessed, she preached. She was an amazing woman and she made each of us strong in so many ways.

"I miss Elvis, Uncle Vernon, Grandma, my aunts and my mother very much," Donna says. "I always shall carry them with me in my heart and mind."

Vester, the only surviving Presley child, "is still alive and kicking," Donna says. He lives in Whitehaven and goes to Graceland every day. His daughter, Patsy, and her family live in Whitehaven as well and she recently became a grandmother.

Priscilla has established herself as an actress and has a successful career now. Lisa Marie has plans to launch a singing career of her own. "Lisa Marie goes back to Graceland sometimes and it's right that she should," Donna says. "Her daddy lived there. I don't talk to Lisa that often and I don't know all the details of her life. People seem to find that hard to believe, but how many of your cousins do you know every little thing about? The thing is, I wish her well. I want her to be happy and that's what Elvis would have wanted too."

Donna and Buddy have moved to Wynne, into an addition they built onto Earl's house, to be near Earl and Susie.

"Since my dad has a bad heart and my sister isn't in good health, we felt that it was best for us to be with them. And it was best, it brought us closer after Mom's death," Donna says. "I was able to really get to know my dad and my sister after being away from them having my own family. It gives me a relief knowing that I'm here if they need me. We enjoy being here together. We all love each other very much and we just enjoy life."

For a while, Buddy was on the police force in Wynne. Now he and Donna operate a successful private investigation and security service business. "I do the footwork and Donna does the paperwork," Buddy explains.

Their children, Stacy and Jamie, both are grown. Stacy is married, Donna adds, "and Jamie's still looking for the right person." Both of her sons, she says, "are fine young men. They are our greatest accomplishment, the thing we are proudest of.

"I like spending time with my family. We don't have to be doing anything special," she says. "I just like being alive and I'm thankful for all of life's blessings. I've got a wonderful family and some really good friends. I'm truly blessed."

Edie lives with her son, Linc, near Birmingham, Alabama. She's done a lot of the things she and Elvis talked about her doing. Although she has had to overcome serious health problems, she has appeared in nationally syndicated commercials and on the daytime drama *As The World Turns*.

Edie also has created a number of programs to benefit causes dear to her heart. The EVE Foundation is a group that deals with environmental issues; ACCESS is a special program to aid victims of national disasters and Positive

Perspectives is a tape and seminar series focusing on confidence development, teamwork and social interaction in the workplace.

She is a sought-after speaker on women's health issues and has been president of her own company for more than 20 years.

Neither Donna nor Edie goes to Graceland now. "After Grandma died, everything changed," Donna says. "It feels oppressive and depressing now, everything that was our reason to be there is gone. It seems odd that a place that had been so much fun and so full of life and vigor could seem so lonely and sad and oppressive."

The cousins have learned that memories don't live in a place, they live in people. They don't find it necessary to go to Graceland to remember their cousin. Anywhere they are, they have their precious memories of Elvis.

Postscript

"We all have weaknesses within us,
it's just how we choose to deal with them
that makes us who we are."
— Donna Presley Early

ELVIS PRESLEY'S FAMILY IS a paradox. On the one hand, no different from any other family. On the other, unlike any other family.

All families have black sheep and heroes. They all have people who are talented and those who, as they say in the South, were behind the door when God was handing out talent.

The thing that made Elvis' family different was Elvis. Other families with the same things going on in their lives didn't have Elvis Presley and his image to contend with as well. Whether it was good or bad, happy or tragic, if it happened to someone in Elvis' family, it was news. Their tragedies made it to tabloids in check-out lines all over America. Their triumphs usually were relegated to fan magazines and newsletters. Everything they did was magnified, often beyond any logical proportion.

The one thing the Presley family didn't share was a universal coping mechanism. Each one had to develop his own. For some, it meant perpetuating bad habits. For others, it meant staying as far away from those habits as possible.

"The Presley family wasn't a dysfunctional family," Donna says. "I hate that word dysfunctional. Too many people use that word as an excuse. The way you were brought up does affect your life, but there comes a time when you have to step up and decide you're an adult and take responsibility for your own actions. You have to stop blaming others.

"The family had problems. Every family has problems. We all have weaknesses within us, it's just how we choose to deal with them that makes us who we are."

One thing is certain. All of Minnie and Jesse Presley's children grew up with a skewed look at marriage and family. It seems that at first Minnie tried to pretend everything was fine with her marriage to Jesse. Nash's school experiences and Jesse's inability to change ended that, however. From that point on, Minnie seemed determined to cope with her husband's drinking and philandering by throwing herself into the job of raising her family. Relying heavily on her deep religious beliefs, she took charge of her children's lives.

She instilled in them a faith in God and a belief in prayer. Through these beliefs and values, she hoped, they would be able to cope with the temptations and problems they would face.

And Minnie had lived through enough to know that her children and their children would face problems. Even though she couldn't have foreseen what an enormous success one of her grandchildren would become and how that success would mean extra pressures for his family, she knew that, as Donna puts it, "bad times are no respecters of persons."

"We all," Susie says, "have our own demons. Insecurity was one of Elvis'.

"It's very prominent in our family. Even though Elvis was secure in his professional life, I believe he was insecure in his personal life.

"I think that not being able to trust is another family trait. I can imagine how Elvis felt. He was very insecure in the fact that he didn't know who really loved him for himself and who didn't. I don't think Elvis was comfortable a lot of times in a one-on-one situation with people. I feel that he became vulnerable when he let himself be known as Elvis the man instead of Elvis the star.

"There's a big difference in being an image and being a real person. The image is easy because you get into such a groove, doing that year after year, it's almost like a second personality to you. But when he sat down with people and they could see into him personally, that's when it got scary for him. And I think he withdrew a lot of times."

Susie says she felt that Elvis used prescription drugs as a way to escape reality.

"When he isolated himself," she adds, "I don't think it was because he hated people. I think it was because he didn't understand himself at the time. He always had been in control of his life and all of a sudden he found himself in a position where his physical condition made him vulnerable to people. When you are physically ill, you are weak. And the drugs impaired his thinking even more."

Insecurity, it seems, also was one of Gladys Smith Presley's demons. "I was just a young child when Aunt Gladys (Elvis' mother) died," Donna says, "but I remember vividly some of the stories that other family members would tell about her drinking problem.

"They talked about how angry she became, due to her drinking, over things as small as a telephone call or if someone said unkind remarks about Elvis on the television or radio.

"Grandma told me that Uncle Vernon was praying one day and Gladys became loud and screamed at him because he was praying. Maybe she felt he was praying for her because of her drinking.

"I don't know why, but she really felt she needed the alcohol. Maybe it was the fact that she already had lost one child and now the call of his career and lifestyle was taking

Elvis away from her. Aunt Gladys was very protective of Elvis and all those she loved."

That love and protective instinct seemed to be a part of the Presley family heritage. "Real warmth and caring is a family trait," Donna says. "We have no trouble saying 'I love you.' It's just as natural as breathing."

"We're just affectionate," Susie adds, "and we love each other even though family members may be halfway around the world. Or even if we've never met them before."

The Presley side of the family wasn't the only branch of the family tree that seemed to have gotten both the good and bad traits that so vividly marked Elvis' life, according to Edie.

Music was a way of life for her family, she says. "My uncles would sing while they worked at my grandfather's sawmill. My grandmother and Minnie would sing when they would go fishing. You'd even hear singing while they were milking the cows."

Edie's uncles, the Hacker Brothers, and other family members became entertainers — performing as well as writing music for other country singers.

"There were eight of those boys and five of them were entertainers who did some writing for Tammy Wynette and George Jones," she says.

Family reunions of the Hoods and Hackers, Edie recalls, were more like concerts than anything else. "We would have these reunions on my grandparents' farm in Northwest Alabama," she explains. "Of course, Minnie sometimes would come because she and my grandmother were more like sisters than like aunt and niece. And, before he was well-known, Elvis would come with Minnie and Vernon to visit with Harrison and Ader Hood.

"All the Hacker brothers and other relatives of Elvis would sit on the big front porch there and play music. And all the other family members would just be scattered all over the yard listening."

As did most things that involved Elvis, the family reunions changed after his career began to take off. Before long, it wasn't just the family at the family reunions. "There would be all these other people that lived around there, all driving by the farm in their cars, hoping Elvis would be there," Edie says.

"My mother's brothers Hartty and W.C. looked a lot like Elvis. I can remember going to the grocery store when we lived in Cleveland, Ohio, and watching the women tear my Uncle W.C.'s shirt off because they thought he was Elvis," she laughs. "The whole time he was trying to tell them that he wasn't Elvis, that he was Elvis' cousin, they were saying, 'Yeah, sure' and tearing his jacket and shirt off. It was snowing and there he was standing in the snow with no jacket and no shirt."

Members of Edie's family shared the Elvis look and the family love of music. They shared some of the other things as well. "My mother had what they called 'bad nerves' back then," Edie explains. "And she spent a lot of time in bed with headaches." Once, she says, she talked to Elvis about her mother's illnesses. "He told me not to worry about it, he said his mother had 'bad nerves,' too," she says. "It probably just was that neither of them knew how to cope with what was going on in her world."

When Edie's parents divorced, her mother left Alabama to move to Indiana where her sister Jackie lived. This gave Edie the opportunity to spend her summers with her Aunt Jackie, who introduced her to singing gospel music at the Medina Temple in Chicago.

Music and entertaining seemed to come naturally to the people in every part of the family. Unfortunately, Edie adds, so did some other traits. While some family members lost themselves in their music, others lost themselves in alcohol and drugs. For some, it cut short promising musical careers. For others, it cut short life.

"Ten years after my brother David died, my brother Phillip was killed in an automobile accident," Edie says. "Phillip had started drinking early in his life. By the time he was about 14 years old he was drinking heavily.

"He married an older woman and they had a daughter

together. His wife left him when the baby was about six months old. He told me he couldn't handle things in his life, his wife leaving and everything. He tried three times to commit suicide.

"Then three months before he died, his car broke down near a little country church. It was raining that night and he decided to walk to the church. The people there that night told me later that he was sober, but you could tell he was coming down off a high.

"But he told them that he wanted to quit drinking, that he wanted to do right. They said they stayed and prayed late with him that night. A few months later, the preacher of that church preached my brother's funeral. He told me that Phillip had touched him that night when he came in and said he wanted to change his life.

"After all that, he was killed in a car wreck. Somebody else was driving. My dad called me late that night and said, 'Edith, Phillip's dead. Your mother can't cope.' I went and made all the funeral arrangements for Phillip, just like I did for David.

"But there was one thing I learned at a very early age from the Presley family — you learned to build on courage, courage to face the world."

A lot of that courage, she says, came from deep religious beliefs the family shared. "One thing we had was an instilled faith in God," she says. "We always knew when everything else failed that He was our best friend. It didn't change everything, but it helped you meet your challenges. This family has loyalty and bonding. We have always believed in prayer and had a strong faith in God."

In the Presley family, Donna says, children always were taught that the only time they failed was when they didn't try. "We were taught to find what we can within ourselves, to build on that, to not be afraid to take a chance," she explains. "My mother would get on to me faster about saying, 'I can't,' than anything. That would infuriate her so much. If any of her children said, 'Mama, I can't do that,' she would get angry with us and say, 'You can do it if you try!' "

Family members learned to focus on the good things and make the best of the bad things, she says. "The bad things are what mold us and make us, you know. The gold has to go through the fire before it can be made into a beautiful pot. Every negative action, every negative thing that we go through, no matter how hurtful or painful at the time, can mold us and make us better people, especially if we let the Lord guide us and direct us.

"The Presley family has the same problems and misunderstandings that other families do," Donna says. "But this is how we worked through them and how we've been able to go on through life and to come out, not just to survive, but to come out on top and be winners.

"What I want everyone to remember when they think about Elvis or Uncle Vernon or my grandmother or my mother — no matter what you've read or seen or heard — is that they had a happiness and an abiding faith, things they in turn brought to other people's lives. Elvis gave to his family as a man and he gave to his fans as an entertainer. I want people to think about how much fun they had when they saw Elvis' movies, what they were doing when they first heard one of his songs. And, above all, to remember the love and happiness Elvis gave to each of you."

Donna Presley Early

Donna Early is the daughter of the singer's beloved Aunt "Nash." Nash, the youngest sister of Elvis' father, cared for the young Elvis when he was growing up and was his friend and advisor until his death.

Donna spent her summers at Graceland when she was a teenager, growing up with and becoming a good friend of Priscilla Beaulieu Presley. She, Priscilla and Elvis all spent quality family time with Elvis' grandmother Minnie Presley, who lived at Graceland. After Elvis' death, Donna became a Graceland employee, answering fan mail for a number of years.

Donna is married to Buddy Early and has two grown sons, Stacy and Jamie. She and Buddy, once a security guard at Graceland, own a security and private investigation business in Wynne, Arkansas. Donna also has worked as a model and as a personnel trainer for a national department store chain.

Donna and Buddy live with her father, who worked for Elvis as Graceland's maintenance supervisor for 20 years, and her sister, Karen Sue (Susie), who was the VIP and Media Tour Guide at Graceland for many years.

Edie Hand

Edie Hand spent a lot of time at Graceland when she was a teenager and a young adult. She sought Elvis' advice as she began planning for her own career in show business. She also was one of the many cousins who had the sometimes challenging assignment of babysitting with Lisa Marie.

Today Edie is a professional entertainer and has appeared in nationally syndicated commercials and on the daytime drama *As The World Turns*. She has been a guest on a number of national and international talk shows, discussing Elvis and his family. She created the EVE Foundation, a group that deals with environmental issues; ACCESS, a special program to aid victims of national disasters, and Positive Perspectives, a tape and seminar series focusing on confidence development, teamwork and social interaction in the workplace. She is a sought-after speaker on women's health issues and has been president of her own company for more than 20 years.

A graduate of the University of North Alabama, she is a member of American Women in Radio and Television, Business and Professional Women, National Speakers' Association, American Cancer Foundation, Sierra Club, National Wildlife Association and Nature Conservancy. Today, she heads her own marketing and seminar development company.

Edie and her son, Linc, live near Birmingham, Alabama.

Lynn Edge

Based in Birmingham, Alabama, Lynn Edge is a veteran writer who spent a number of years as a reporter for *The Birmingham News* before she became a freelance writer. While at *The News*, she won the Associated Press Newswriting Award for Spot News coverage of a sniper attack in West Birmingham.

She and her husband, Garland Reeves, have two children, Roxanna and Rhett.

LC	9/99